WHEN CHILDREN ASK ABOUT GOD

When Children Ask About God

HAROLD S. KUSHNER

SCHOCKEN BOOKS · NEW YORK

First published by SCHOCKEN BOOKS 1976

Published by arrangement with the Jewish Reconstructionist Foundation, Inc.

© Copyright 1971 by Harold S. Kushner

Library of Congress Cataloging in Publication Data

Kushner, Harold S.
  When children ask about God.

  1. God (Judaism) —Study and teaching.
  2. Jewish religious education of children.
  3. Jewish children—Religious life. I. Title.

[BM610.K85 1976]   296.3'11   76-9140

Manufactured in the United States of America

10 9 8 7 6 5 4 3   81 82

ISBN 0-8052-0549-7

To our children,

AARON ZEV *and* ARIEL ANN

who have taught me more about God
than I have taught them.

Foreword

I have attempted, in this book, to convey some of the ideas that I hold about God which are suitable for communicating to young children, ages 4-14, and to offer reasonable, non-supernatural alternatives to some of the familiar ways in which the idea of God is often presented, ways which so many parents have difficulty offering seriously to their children, and which may in fact be harmful to a child's religious development. The ideas you will encounter here are mine in the sense that I believe them and would be willing to defend them, not in the sense that I created them out of my own resources. Those readers who are familiar with the thought of Mordecai M. Kaplan will recognize the degree to which this book and its author are indebted to him beyond all formal acknowledgement. Dr. Kaplan's program of Reconstructionism and his naturalistic theology have provided me with a framework for understanding and explaining Judaism since my first days as his student at the Jewish Theological Seminary in 1955. This volume is in large measure an effort to translate some of his theological ideas into forms suitable for parent-child conversation. I can only hope that his insights have been conveyed faithfully, and that the book meets his high standards of intellectual and spiritual honesty.

Rabbi Ira Eisenstein of the Jewish Reconstructionist Foundation and the Reconstructionist Press has been a faithful, patient and immensely helpful guide and editor. Only he and I are aware of how much this book has been helped by his advice.

I have also benefited greatly from the studies of Jean Piaget and his school, exploring how the mind of a child develops and how a child perceives the world around him at various ages. It was a reading of Piaget's *The Moral Judgment of the Child* which prompted me to postulate the stages our perception of God undergoes as we mature, as I have developed it in this volume.

Those readers familiar with the field of social psychology will recognize my indebtedness to Erik Erikson as well, especially for his outline of the psychic needs of the young child for such qualities as trust and competence in his early years.

In the field of teaching religion to young children, one name stands out, that of Dr. Sophia Lyons Fahs, whose works I have read with great profit. Although my own experiences and my specifically Jewish orientation often led me to conclusions different from hers, her impact on the tone of this book must be acknowledged. In the course of this work, I also encountered the valuable work being done in England by Ronald Goldman, and have not hesitated to make use of his insights.

Among Jewish authors, Rabbis Roland Gittelsohn and David Cedarbaum have taught me much about the areas with which this book is concerned, and Rabbi Gittelsohn paid me the additional courtesy of reading the manuscript in its early stages and offering several valuable suggestions.

Many of the ideas I set forth in the pages of this book are new, and may seem radical, though many have already been suggested by sages of the past whose traditional piety and scholarship far exceeded my own. Many of my teachers have had a hand in bringing me to the conclusions embodied in this volume, including some whose personal theological stance is very far from the one here offered. I hope I have been faithful to what they taught me.

And a last profound acknowledgement goes to those members of the congregations which I served in Great Neck, New York and Natick, Massachusetts, for responding to these ideas as I presented them, criticizing them where they were weak or imprecise, and reassuring me that they made sense, indeed that, for the first time, religion made sense because of the theological framework in which I ventured to cast it. From all these sources have I drawn the ideas about God, the world, and the Jewish people, as I have tried, however imperfectly, to spell them out in these pages.

RABBI HAROLD S. KUSHNER

Natick, Mass.

TABLE OF CONTENTS

WHEN CHILDREN ASK ABOUT GOD

Chapter I

INTRODUCTION

THIS BOOK IS DESIGNED to help parents and teachers answer children's questions about God. I undertook the writing of it with some trepidation, because I felt I knew little about God and only a little more about children. I undertook it, nonetheless, with the encouragement of Rabbi Ira Eisenstein, of the Reconstructionist Press, and with the assurance of many friends and congregants that such a book is welcome and necessary. Ultimately, the book turned out to be less about God, and more about life—its problems and promises—and about people—their needs and hopes, their fears and dreams. It became a book revolving around the fact that children and their parents ask questions about the world, sometimes falling in love with it, basking in its sunshine, enjoying its gifts, and wanting to know more about it—sometimes cruelly hurt by it and wondering why. They want to understand the world and their own place in it. "God" is a convenient, time-honored code-word for discussing the problems and promises of being alive and human in this world, a term which lends our discussion a great deal of emotional momentum and a continuity with the past.

A word might be in order about what this book is and what it is not about: it is not a theological *Dr. Spock,* a chronological guide to the stages through which your child will pass, listing the questions he will ask at every age. That is far too unpredictable and individual a matter. Some children will pose few of the problems discussed in this book; others will ask questions neither I nor the publishers ever formulated. It is not a book to which you can run when a question comes up and consult for a handy, capsulized answer. I hope that the reader will digest this book and make its answers his own, so that he can speak with personal commitment and authenticity and that the child will be given his father's answers in his father's words.

Neither is this a book for the parent believing firmly in a God who made the world in six days, dictated the Scriptures to Moses and causes all that happens in the world, rewarding the good and punishing the disobedient. If you are such a parent and your only problem is in getting your child to believe as firmly and wholeheartedly as you do, there are books to help you bridge that gap, but this is not one of them.

This book is for the parents and teachers who are inevitably confronted with questions about God and His world, about good and evil, reward and punishment and immortality, and who are dissatisfied with the answers they themselves received as children from their own parents and teachers. It is easy enough to give a child a simple, pious answer and solve" the immediate problem, only to find a few years later that you have a child who believes all religion to be fatuous nonsense. It is easy to say to a child that "we are not permitted to question the way God runs His world," but harder to live with the implications of that answer. I could never be happy giving an answer like that and no child of average curiosity and intellectual restlessness should be willing to accept it. Not only is it self-defeating to speak in this vein to a child whose secular education teaches him to probe, to test and to question but it is poor Judaism as well. Shall Judaism, the religion whose Scriptures portray Abraham challenging God's justice on behalf of the men of Sodom and Job questioning God's concern for men, the religion that gave the world Spinoza, Freud, and Einstein, suddenly put up intellectual *No Trespassing* signs at the borders of every sensitive area?

There are a great many times when, speaking of God, we have to say, "We don't know for sure and we may never know," but we can never relinquish our right to question, or to compare the intuitions of the ancients with the empirical facts of our own experience.

This is a book not for children, but for parents. It intends to give you a consistent point of view to accept as your own, if you so choose, and to share with your children. It need hardly be said that my answers are not the only answers, but they are one set of answers which make sense to me and which have made sense to people with whom I have shared them. They avoid some of the most serious pitfalls of teaching—those which offer children shallow and even harmful ideas about God, ideas that elicit either fear or scorn or both. I have tried to convey a reasonable, essentially humanistic understanding of what God can mean to us, within the framework of the Jewish tradition—an understanding which can command

both intellectual respect and profound moral commitment. I have tried to explore how this idea of God can be
communicated to children at various stages of their
spiritual development. Even as it was the mandate of the
prophet Jeremiah *"to pluck up and tear down, to destroy
and to overthrow, to build and to plant,"* so did I find that
my task called for two portions of negative content—the
uprooting of old ideas and insisting on what God is not—
for every portion of affirmation. There are good reasons
for this: I have a tentative notion as to what God is, but
I feel much more strongly about the things He is not
and does not do.

There is something wrong with a religion or concept
of God which emphasizes fear and guilt. Human beings
are not meant to live in cowering fear and meek submis-
sion. They cannot live fully, humanly, if they are constantly
obsessed by the worry that they have broken some rule
and lost the love of their parents, their religious leaders,
or God. In its extreme form, such a religion produces
people who do nothing, or at least do nothing on their
own initiative, as a way of avoiding sin. In less extreme
form, this religion makes the world a dark, dour, cruel
and cheerless place, wherein obsession with sin drives out
dreams of accomplishment and fear of punishment over-
shadows hope of reward.

There is something wrong with a religion or concept
of God which fosters in our hearts unrealistic expectations of the world, telling us, for example, that no harm
comes to good people, that we get only what we deserve,
that sincere prayers will be answered. All of this is simply

not true and the child who is taught that it is will end up incapable of believing in himself, his parents, his religion, or God. One minister has written that for the first twenty years of his ministry he taught his flock that God was a loving father who would take care of them... and that now he has to spend his time explaining to these same people why He hasn't.

And there is something wrong with a religion or a God-concept which tells us that it is somehow improper to ask questions. If human intelligence, curiosity and the capacity for outrage in the presence of injustice are qualities God has given us, how can it be an act of disloyalty to God to use these qualities in seeking answers to some of the most important questions about life? It is certainly desirable for us to have faith in God. But faith in God does not mean closing our eyes to questions and conflicts. It does not mean believing that "whatever is, is right" and that "whatever happens is God's will." Faith in God means believing in God's world, believing that we need not be afraid to examine it closely for however much we come to learn about it, it will still turn out to be an essentially orderly and benevolent place. It means believing in Man, in the mind God gave him to explore and understand life and in the soul God gave him to sanctify what he discovers.

Whatever God may be, I cannot believe that He stands for obsessive guilt, false expectations, and artificial ignorance.

And even here, in our emphasis on what God is not, we are on good, traditional Jewish ground. The great medieval Jewish philosopher Maimonides warns us that we can speak accurately about God only when we speak negatively. We can say what God is not, but as soon as we try to affirm God and speak of what He is, we are compelled to become metaphoric and slightly misleading and inaccurate. We have no choice but to use human language, human terms of reference in regard to an other-than-human God. Can we say that God exists? Yes, but not in the same way that we say a man or a tree exists. To say that God exists is only a less cumbersome way of saying that, whatever He is, He is *not* imaginary, *not* a bit of wishful thinking or a figment of our imagination. Does God hear prayer? He may or He may not, but if He does, it is certainly not by the same physical mechanism that you and I hear.

And yet we have to talk about God, what He is as well as what He is not. We cannot avoid it. Even if we try to cleanse our speech of any reference to Him, saying to ourselves that since all "God-talk" is misleading and inaccurate, we won't talk about Him at all, we will not succeed. Some people have suggested that for the first few years of religious education we should concentrate on life experiences without introducing the name of God and the inevitable oversimplifications and abstractions by which we try to explain that word. While the idea has a certain theoretical plausibility and would avoid problems which probably cannot be solved to our total satisfaction, it is probably unrealistic. Our children don't exist in a hermetically-sealed environment. They live in a culture where the word "God" is frequently invoked. Even if we were to force ourselves to use clumsy circumlocutions in discussing the nature and purpose of Man, the basis of his ethical behavior, consolation of the bereaved—so as not to mention God—our culture would trip us up.

With a child's first visit to the synagogue, his first "unexpurgated" Bible story, the name of God will arise. And if radio and television programs don't raise the issue, complete with confusing imagery and (from our point of view) misinformation, our children's playmates will. There are few sources of information as misinformed and as positive about their misinformation as young children inventing their own answers to the questions that perplex them, questions for which their parents have not supplied answers.

In this book, we will suggest an understanding of the word "God" which is different from the ways most people understand the word. Are we justified in continuing to use the same word, making it mean what we take it to mean, when other people use it to mean something else? Such usage would seem legitimate and proper on at least two grounds. First of all, the word "God" and the whole vocabulary of words we apply to the divine, have stood for many different things in human history. Their meaning has changed often. Our Hebrew ancestors used the word *Elohim* to refer to the invisible, intangible Creator of the world, Who brought them out of Egypt and gave them the *Torah,* at the same time that their pagan neighbors were using the same word to refer to statues, trees and stones, or to the natural forces of rainfall, harvest, and reproduction. In ancient Greece and Rome, in medieval

Europe and in our own time, the philosophers have had one sort of meaning in mind when they spoke of "God," while the man in the street had another—and yet both used the same word. No one can say that the word "God" has always had a single, fixed meaning.

And secondly, though we may define God differently, though we may differ from the conventional understanding of His attributes, there is a very close connection in meaning and function between what the term "God" means to us and what it means, and has meant, to the average believer. We, as they, are referring to the Power that creates life and gives it meaning. We, as they, are talking about the Ultimate Guarantor of our aspirations, the Power that calls upon us to be moral. Why then should we have to discard a vocabulary so rich in emotional connotation and evocative power, so closely associated to what men over the ages have learned about living and start from scratch to invent a new series of terms, which later generations will have to replace, in turn, as their understanding of the world grows beyond ours? We are not starting a new enterprise. We are continuing the effort to understand Man's world, in which religion has always been involved, and for which purpose it has developed a special, highly meaningful vocabulary.

In sum, we have no choice but to speak to our children of God. We must, because they will ask us about Him; and even without asking, they will be curious about Him and profoundly troubled by theological questions (phrased, of course, in their own terms and at their own level). We must, because if we don't speak of Him, our children are liable to fall into one of two undesirable patterns. They may accept some of the simple-minded notions about God which are current in much of our society, notions which I consider inaccurate, intellectually compromising, and psychologically harmful simply to fill a vacuum. Or else, if they have the good sense and sensitivity to reject them, they may reject belief in God entirely and commit themselves to a life in which some of the most precious and valuable aspects of human existence are missing.

Do these last lines sound vaguely like the introduction to a book on "the birds and the bees?"—"Teach your child the right attitudes, or he will pick up the wrong ones from his playmates." The resemblance may not be that far-fetched. There was a time (is it over?) when parents couldn't speak to their children about sex and reproduction, because they themselves were confused and uncertain. They left their children with an informational-emotional vacuum, which became filled with every kind of distortion, fear, and fantasy. Until recently, this problem didn't exist for the Jew teaching his child about God, because he had a clear and confident sense of what he believed. Those of us who can remember Orthodox grandparents of unshaken piety may envy them for the wholemindedness of their faith and the uncomplicated clarity of their beliefs, even as we realize that we know too much about the world to go back to their way of seeing it. But if people who have attained enlightened, healthy attitudes about sex and reproduction have available to them a wealth of material for teaching their children that "the stork didn't bring them," we are still confused and uncertain about God and have very little guidance in giving our children something to believe in and hold on to. It was dismaying to find, in preparing this text, how little there was available for parents and teachers who are looking for help in presenting this point of view, or one like it, to children. This book is an attempt to fill that gap. It starts with a premise which I hope my readers will share: *it should be a primary concern of religion to make a person trust the world and like himself.* Sometimes the world will turn out to be unreliable, and religion will have to explain and console. Sometimes a person will have good reason to be disappointed in himself, his behavior, his priorities. But basically, religion ought to help a person feel good about himself. Yet, as this book began to take shape, it occurred to me that some traditional modes of speaking about God fostered feelings of guilt and unworthiness. To my mind, that is bad religion. I have seen too many lives blighted by a compulsive sense of guilt over perfectly normal thoughts and deeds.

Why should religion cede to other disciplines such fundamentally religious words as "love," "trust," "belonging," and limit its own vocabulary to "sin" and "judgment"?

Chapter II

IF GOD ISN'T A BEARDED OLD MAN IN THE SKY, WHAT IS HE?

THE MAJOR PART OF OUR TASK of teaching children about God can be summed up in two not-so-simple steps. First, we must come to a clear understanding of what we ourselves are ready to believe about God. And then, we have to translate this concept into "words of one syllable," geared for a child's understanding.

There is more to it than that, of course. There are aspects of belief a child needs at one stage which he will later outgrow. There are ideas which may be valid, even necessary, for us, but too subtle or abstract for a young child's mind. There are ideas and images which are not literally true, but which enrich the imagination. We will have to consider the advisability of using them. But once we have completed the first two steps mentioned above, we will be more than halfway home.

Thus, in 1956, Mordecai Kaplan wrote:

"To answer any difficult question raised by a child, two requirements are necessary: (1) the ability to answer the question to the satisfaction of an adult, and (2) the ability to adapt that answer to a child's mind in accordance with his age. The main difficulty in answering this question (about God and illness) is that we have

11

not yet arrived at an answer that is fully satisfying to the modern adult mind." (*Question Jews
Ask,* p.117)

What can a modern adult believe about God in his
own mind, before he tries to convey his belief to his
child? Let us begin negatively, with some things God
is not.

*"Thou shalt not make unto thee a graven image, nor
any manner or likeness of any thing that is in the heaven
above, or that is in the earth below, or that is in the water
under the earth."* (Exodus 20:4)

If the Second Commandment teaches us anything, it
teaches us that *God is not a thing.* We are to make no
visual representation of Him, not because it would offend
His dignity to have His portrait done poorly, but because
He does not lend Himself to pictorial representation.
He is totally different from the three-dimensional
animal-vegetable-mineral world in whose terms we are
accustomed to think. We cannot see Him, not because
He is *invisible,* but because He is *intangible.* He has no
form, He does not fill space and therefore (as we will
have the opportunity to discuss later) the question of His
being in one place and not in another is misleading and
almost meaningless. God is not a thing—He has none of
the physical properties of things.

This is one reason why, as I wrote in the Introduction,
all discussion of God in human, thing-oriented language
is bound to be metaphorical and misleading if taken
literally. Does God hear prayers and cries? Human beings
and animals hear because of the reverberations of sound

waves on the organs of their inner ears. If God hears, He certainly doesn't hear that way. Whatever else I believe about God, I can't believe that He has bones and cartilage in His ears the way we do. Does God know our thoughts? Is He pleased or angered by them? For human beings, knowledge involves electrical currents passing between brain cells. Emotional changes involve secretions of the glands. God, removed from the world of "thing-ness," has neither brain cells nor adrenal glands. "God's knowledge," "God's wrath," "pleasing in the sight of God"... must be understood as poetic metaphors and not taken literally as implying anything about God's nature.

And yet, I would plead for the right to continue using such metaphors, open to misconception as they may be. Our language and conversation would be improverished beyond repair if our every utterance had to meet the stringent requirements of a logician and linguistic analyst. We permit ourselves to speak of sunrise and sunset, though we know well enough that the sun neither rises nor sets, but that our corner of the earth moves toward it or away from it. The poet Lovelace can write *"When Love with unconfined wings hovers within my gates..."* we can send greeting cards with Cupids on them, yet no one suspects us of being pagan animists who really believe that Love is a winged cherub with a bow and arrow. We recognize these as poetic usages that appeal to the imagination. Similarly, we should be free to speak of "God's creating," "God's caring," "God's inspiring the doctor and scientist," without being taken to mean a God who is a Heaven-dwelling Superman, a God who is actually "doing" these things with real hands and real bodily organs. We have no language other than this language by which to speak of God and we must speak of Him.

Let us agree then that we will continue speaking of God and use traditional forms of expression, with the understanding that we are not obliged to take them literally or be held accountable for the strict connotations of the word, as long as these expressions do not lead us astray. Let us give ourselves the same freedom of expression we extend to the weatherman, who is free to speak of sunrise and sunset as much as he wishes—as long as he doesn't base his forecast on the theory that the sun moves around the earth.

If God is not a thing, it goes without saying that He is not a person, nor even a superperson. Despite Michaelangelo God does not resemble anyone's musclebound grandfather. He does not "do what people do, only better." He is a totally different order of reality than we humans are, not just bigger, better, or further away, but completely *different*.

Yet so much of the confusion, so many of the misunderstandings about God stem from this habit of thinking of Him as a pious Superman, subject to no limitation, not even to the laws of Nature. "Why did God do that?" "How could He let it happen?" "Don't you believe that God *told* us this is wrong, and *wants* us not to do it?" Perhaps the greatest step toward a mature understanding of God is the realization that God doesn't "do" things the way a person does them. He doesn't "cause" things to happen in the world, except in a special sense of the word, different from the way we use it about ourselves when we speak of our "causing" things to happen or our "making" things. It would be very pleasant to believe in a God who really did make things happen by the same rational and physical processes that we employ, a God who punished us for what we did wrong and protected us from harm if we deserved protection. But there is so much evidence from real experience contradicting this kind of belief that its proponent would have to spend all his time defending and apologizing for it.

If God is not a person or a thing, if He has neither shape or form and does not take up space, what is He? There is probably no completely accurate word in our language, for the reasons we have already mentioned. In order not to mislead, we would need a word used only for God, not for any tangible, earth-bound object and then we would have no basis for understanding that word. As a matter of fact, we have such a word—"God"—and we have difficulty understanding what we mean by it because there are no other things on earth to which we can apply it. But there are, however, words that point in the right direction. God is something like a Force, a Power, a Process, a quality of relationship. God is the name we attach to the fact that we find certain things possible and meaningful in the world and in our lives and the fact that we find ourselves stirred to move in the direction of realizing these possibilities. We call God the force behind our growing and learning, our curiosity to discover and our impulse to share and to help.

The name "God" stands for all those qualities in the world and in ourselves which our religious tradition labels as divine, that is, as comprising full human spiritual development, fashioning Man into what he is at his best and most fully realized. If Truth, Justice, Mercy, Generosity, Love are among the things we need to be genuine human beings, to be, in the Biblical phrase, men *"in God's image"*, then the name "God" stands for the existence of these qualities in the world and the existence of a corresponding impulse toward them in every human soul.

The statement, for example, that "God is just" or that "God demands justice of men" doesn't really tell us anything about a being named God. But it does tell us that justice is one of the qualities human beings need to be fully and satisfyingly human. It tells us that we cannot realize our potential greatness as human beings *unless* we practice justice and are part of a just society. And it tells us further that justice is possible in this world, that the world around us and the human soul within us are not constructed so as to mock our strivings for justice from the outset. The same process of interpretation holds for all the other qualities for which the name of God stands. Belief in God is not so much a statement about Somebody living in Heaven as it is an affirmation of the world and the human beings who inhabit it, what they are and what they are capable of becoming. Belief in God means believing that the universe has order and direction, that it encourages human goodness and moral growth and that the impulse each of us feels to be a good person is a reflection of the purposefulness existing in the cosmos at large.

Some years back, a Soviet cosmonaut emerged from his space capsule and announced triumphantly that he had circled the earth several dozen times without bumping into God or any of His angels. He thought he was proving that God didn't exist and that religion was therefore false. Actually, he was only noting that God was not a thing, an object occupying space with which a spaceship might collide. But if we understand "God" to mean, among other things, the Power that awakens in men the curiosity to explore the universe, that plants in them the potential for scientific genius, that gives them the courage to face danger and risk their lives in outer space in an effort to expand the boundaries of human knowledge and mastery of the world, might we not say that the astronauts have "bumped into God" and seen Him "face to face" *more* than the average person?

May I emphasize at this point that God is *no less real* for not being a thing or a person. A force can be real. An idea can have reality; it can affect and change the world by its operation. No one would claim that electricity, heat, fire are imaginary because they are not *things*, but are forces and processes that operate through their effect on other, more tangible objects. Nor would anyone say that love and courage are unreal because you can't keep them in a box and take them out to show people.

Ideas may be false and love may, at times, be unrealistic, if they do not conform to the way things are in the world. But a valid idea can be as "real" as a tree, if not more so, in its capacity to shape and influence people's lives. In this sense, an intangible God can be real without having form or taking up space, if the attributes for which He stands are real and valid in our world. If we use the word "God" to designate such qualities as Justice, Love and Truth and if Justice, Love and Truth are imaginary and incapable of being realized, if they do not and cannot exist in this world then God too would be imaginary. But if Justice, Love and Truth *are* real, if they are at least possible, then God too is real and not a result of wishful thinking or the product of our imagination.

To be sure, there is an emotional as well as a psychological wrench in reshaping the ways we think and speak about God. Some of my best friends are sure that I am an atheist because of my convictions about God; in a sense, they are right. There are a great many "gods" I *don't* believe in, and *only one* in Whom I do. There are concepts of God other people hold in all sincerity which I cannot accept. Ideas about God which I once believed are no longer mine. We are all "atheists" of that stripe, rejecting most of the alternative ideas about God that are offered us and searching for the one which we will be able to believe and upon which we can base our view of the world.

In the process of developing a mature idea of God, there are stages through which we pass. There are beliefs about God which we accept when we are children and later outgrow, even as there are conceptions of God which mankind as a whole held when the human race was younger, which it is now outgrowing.

The ways in which people understood the term "God" in the past have undergone a process of evolution. Society has outgrown some beliefs and exchanged them for new ones and we find that the course of the change closely parallels the individual's changing concept of authority as he grows up. Young societies conceived of God the way young children conceive of authority in their own world. As societies matured, the meaning of God in their religion changed, with surprising resemblance to the maturing idea of authority in the individual's life.

To the infant, the external world exists for one purpose only: to satisfy his needs—to feed him, keep him warm, and assuage his loneliness and hurt. He is terrified, angered and bewildered when the world around him fails to do so and he looks for ways of forcing its compliance.

As he grows older, he learns that the world around him is not merely an extension of his own ego. It does not exist solely for his benefit, but has its own independent will and existence. It makes demands on him and will not let itself be compelled. The child's parents, who have heretofore been fountains of generosity, are now seen as figures of authority—making demands, telling him what he must do and not do. Their approval can be won only by obedience to these demands. Accompanying this attitude is the child's conviction that external authority is all-wise and all-powerful. External authority will make only legitimate demands and correct any inequities that result, offering proper reward for obedience rendered.

Some people never develop beyond this stage. For the rest of their lives, their point of reference is that om-

niscient, omnipotent external authority. "What should
I do next? If I do something wrong, will I be punished?
Will I lose the favor of those I depend on?"

But there is a level beyond this which a man must
reach if he would be fully mature. He must learn to
internalize the standards of right and wrong by which he
lives. The "still, small voice" which tells him how to
behave should be his *own* voice, not an external command. The mature individual acts not in order to avoid
punishment or win approval, but to maintain his own
integrity. He does things, and abstains from others, because he has accepted certain standards by which he
intends to live. Authority has become for him a commitment from within, not something imposed from above.

The noted Swiss psychologist Jean Piaget, to whom
we shall refer again, has outlined this process of growth
in a masterful study of the development of the sense of
morality in children. Piaget has studied the attitudes of
children toward the rules of the games they play and his
findings bear an amazing resemblance to the stages of
religious belief in the history of human society and to the
evolution of the God-idea in the individual. Young
children see the rules of, for instance, their games of
marbles as "sacred and untouchable...every suggested
alteration strikes the child as a transgression." If children
in other neighborhoods play with different rules, it is
because they "were given different rules" or "don't know
any better." As a child grows older, however, he understands that the rules were established by mutual consent
and the pooling of human wisdom and experience and

can be changed for the benefit of all. At first, he may change them whimsically and arbitrarily, revelling in his new-found power. He may design and play some very silly games until he discovers that they are not very much fun. Very soon, he finds ways of reaching a consensus which ensures fair and satisfying play for all.

"The rules are at first something external to the individual, and... sacred to him. Then as he gradually makes them his own, they come to be felt as the free product of mutual agreement and an autonomous conscience." (Piaget, "The Moral Judgment of the Child," Collier, p.28)

The history of the idea of God in religion follows the same developmental pattern. The gods are at first seen as extensions of a society's ego, existing solely to respond to its needs, to protect people against enemies, to send the rain in its due season, to ensure the harvest. In short, they are perceived very much as a human infant perceives his parents.

They then become the all-knowing, all-powerful author(s) of a moral code. In primitive societies, we find the same lack of distinction between "what we want and need" and "what the world above and beyond us wants or needs," that characterizes the human infant. At the appropriate time, in response to the appropriate cue, the gods supply rain and food, blessing the fruit of the land and the fruit of the womb. The sun rises, the rains come, the crops grow at the behest of a benevolent deity and any break in the pattern leaves the people angry and bewildered—wondering why the gods have stopped smiling. (May one further speculate that the least theological development seems to have taken place in those parts of the world where rain and crops are most abundant— where people have never been brought face to face with the question of why the gods have stopped showering goodness upon them?)

As religion matures and people confront the realities of their situation, the gods are no longer seen as automatic guarantors of weather and fertility. Men learn that rain and crops sometimes fail (even as the child realizes one day that his parents do not yield to his every wish) and realize that the gods make demands upon them and expect certain behavior—be it sacrifices or morality— before they will confer their bounty.

A hint of this transition is perhaps found in the Book of Deuteronomy: *"For the land which you go in to possess is not like the land of Egypt whence you have come, where you sowed your seed and watered it by foot like a vegetable garden* (i.e., where the natural water supply was abundant). *The land you go to possess is a land of hills and valleys, that drinks the rainwater of heaven... The eyes of the Lord are upon it at all times. And if you hearken to My commandments, to love the Lord your God and to serve Him with all your heart and all your soul,* then *I will give your land rain in its season, the early rain and the late rain, that you may harvest your grain, your wine, and your oil."* (Deut.11-10-14) In other words, in Egypt nature *automatically* sees to the food supply, but in Israel, it is *dependent* on the people's behavior and their loyalty to God.

Hebrew monotheism and its derivative religions thus deserve to be called "higher religions," not merely on grounds of personal preference, but because they represent a more advanced, more mature stage in the development of the God-concept. The earlier view of God as the supplier of all wants was supplemented by an understanding of God as making certain rules, certain demands upon His followers.

Unquestioning obedience, however, is not adult maturity; as the individual's attitude toward authority goes beyond compulsive obedience to the mature stage where one lives by autonomous standards of behavior, so can we look for a further, similar development of the God-idea. If our thesis is valid—that society's idea of God parallels the individual's idea of authority—the next stage of the God-idea will be the *internalizing* of what is true and valid in religion, so that the rules we live by are no longer "God's standards imposed upon us," but our own standards, perceived and voluntarily adopted on the basis of experience and rational analysis.

"God" will come to mean that impulse in the human collective and in the universe as a whole corresponding to conscience in the individual, the name given to that force existing in the cosmos and in every one of us which helps us to identify that which is good and true and worthwhile and which moves us to pledge ourselves to live up to it.

"The unity of God" will mean the integrating of all facets of the human soul and all elements of society to work for these goals, so that all men and all nations will know what is good and will work *wholeheartedly* for it, diverting none of their energy to "other gods." God will no longer be thought of as "our Father in Heaven," whose approval we seek to earn, but will be the divine spark in every human being and in every God-oriented community, which impels people to growth and self-fulfilment. God will be, as the Rabbis of the *Talmud* anticipated, the "soul of the world," with a spark of Him in every mature human soul.

There are some people, I know, who will feel disappointed with this definition of God. They might feel: "Is that all there is to Him? Is He just a shorthand term for my capacity to be a good person and the promise that I will find the world in harmony with that capacity? Why, your God comes out to be so much less majestic and awe-inspiring than the God I meet in the pages of of the Bible."

I suppose so. I suppose there is something in each of us that would like to return to a simpler time when an all-wise, all-powerful figure made all the decisions for us and earned our love and loyalty in the process, a time when all we had to do was follow instructions. Certainly the tendency of a whole society in time of crisis to seek out a powerful leader and place the hard decisions on his shoulders would seem to bear this out.

But we know that if we are to grow to our full spiritual stature as human beings, we have to outgrow this habit.

And we realize that if God is not a person, if He is not an object taking up space, He can't strike down the blasphemer, He can't speak to Moses in a voice of thunder (in Hebrew presumably, but with which pronunciation?)—nor can He really "do" any of the things which, in the Bible, characterize Him as a mighty King and Redeemer. That comforting image of an unerring, superpowerful God is one of the things we have to leave behind us as we grow up and get to know the craters and pitfalls of the world in which we live.

Isn't there, however, an inspiration of a more mature order in the satisfactions of love and generosity and accomplishment the world holds in store for us and in the realization that the potential for such satisfaction is found in every one of us, in the knowledge that everyone of us is related to God in that way?

It's hard, I know, to give up the idea that God knows each of us and cares about each of us personally. Many people just cannot part with the idea of a "personal God," a God who relates to us personally. If God is really God, they tell themselves, He will find a way of maintaining all the advantages of being personal without suffering any of the disadvantages. And yet the God in which I believe—God as understood in these pages— *is* in a real sense a personal God; it is not that He *has* personality but that He *affects* people personally. Let me explain what I mean.

Gravity is an impersonal force. If two people fall from the top of a building together, they will both fall downward at the same speed, irrespective of who the people are and why they are falling from a building. Gravity is impersonal, because it affects all people in the same way. But love, justice, charity, beauty, creativity, and all the other qualities we call "divine" are not impersonal forces like gravity. They affect different people *differently* according to the *individual personality* of each. What stirs or inspires one man leaves another cold. Two people go through the same experience; one finds his life transformed by it, the other remains indifferent. This can be equated with God treating us personally, each of us according to his own inner personality. Long ago, the Rabbis suggested that: *"God is like a mirror, which never changes, yet everyone who looks into it sees a different face."* (Pesikta d'Rav Kahana, 109b, quoted in A Rabbinic Anthology, p.6)

One question remains to be considered before we leave these adult concerns and turn to the questions our children ask us about God. Having arrived at a mature, consistent understanding of God, free of superstition and anthropomorphism, how ruthlessly consistent and non-anthropomorphic are we to be with our children? How childish need a child's religion be?

Can we teach them things we ourselves do not exactly believe, things they will one day have to outgrow and unlearn? Do we tell them Bible stories in which God speaks and hears, works miracles and knocks down walls? Do we encourage them to pray for good health, good grades and good weather? To what extent shall we make allowances for the fact that they *are* children and not small adults with adult mental capacities?

The issues here are not only our own honesty and consistency, but the absorptive capacity of our children at various ages. We may anticipate that children, in the course of becoming adults in body, mind, and spirit, will undergo a process of evolution similar to the one I have described, that they will travel the path on which the God-idea evolved as society matured. When they are very young, they will probably picture God in crude, concrete, even contradictory terms; they will collect statements about God the way they collect shells or picture cards, adding each new acquisition to their treasury without seeing whether or not it harmonizes with the others. They will credit God with extravagant size and power and obviously enjoy speaking about Him so, finding a certain satisfaction in announcing that He can do everything and that there are no limits to His strength. There is very little point in trying to correct them. Perhaps the biggest contribution we make during the early years is a negative one. We can do a lot of good by restraining ourselves during this period. If we refrain from reacting with delight to the fact that our child is "showing an interest in religion," if we don't explicitly endorse our children's statements, but hedge about their affirmations with comments like "yes, it's something like that, but not exactly," our task later will be that much easier. During these early years, we can "pull the weeds so that the flowers will grow later," or at least not lend ourselves to the deliberate cultivation of "weeds."

Under a certain age, children are uncomfortable with intangible abstractions. Their minds thirst for the real, the concrete, the vivid and they translate abstractions into tangible entities. Thus they can't comprehend the term Evil, but they know all about "bad guys." When one young girl asked her mother, "Does God have skin?" and was told that He didn't, she replied: "He must look funny without it."

An abstract God–as–the–Power–that–makes–certain–things–happen will mean little to children at an early age. If we try to tell them that God is the name we use for a certain Spirit, *we'll* know what we mean, but our children are liable to walk away thinking that God resembles Casper, the Friendly Ghost. And above all, let us avoid the temptation to talk too much, to inundate a child's curiosity in a flood of words, and to extinguish that natural sense of awe about God that children seem to have and that we adults might well envy.

Our task during these years will be partly to compromise with their limitations and withold answers until the children are ready for them and partly to introduce them to the abstract idea of God as a Power that makes things possible in the most concrete terms we can—such as the growth of a flower, the healing of a bruise, the "smiling inside" feeling of gratitude or self-satisfaction.

Above all, never let us be afraid to say to our children: "That is a very difficult question. People have been trying to answer it for a long time, and they are not sure they know all the answers there are for it. Let me try to answer it as best as I can, but you probably won't understand it all until you're older." Even if we ourselves have settled on answers that satisfy us, it is important to teach children that the questions they ask about God have *not* been answered to the satisfaction of all serious thinkers and that they are very difficult questions. *Let* them know that there is a great deal for them to figure out for themselves as they learn more about the world. In this way, instead of giving them *our* religion, fully developed, we will set the stage for their working out their own. Isn't our own faith more securely ours because *we* worked it out from the material parents and teachers gave us, rather than because we inherited it intact? The Rabbis of the *Midrash* interpreted the words of the prayerbook, *"My God and God of my fathers"* to mean that only *after* we have found God ourselves and formed our own understanding of Him, can we appreciate "the God of our fathers."

As the child grows older, he begins to outgrow his childish conception of God. He is less likely to be thought of a Superperson in the sky and more likely to refer to ideas of right and wrong. Once again, we see how humanity's slow process of religious evolution is recapitulated in the individual child. At about ten, a child will try to sort through the theological baggage that he has accumulated over several years of asking questions and hearing stories. He is aware of contradictions and impossibilities. At this point our answers can do the most good. They can recast ideas held from childhood into acceptable terms and help the child sort through ideas worth holding and childish notions he is now ready to outgrow; they can encourage him to question and provide him with explanations that make sense to him. He will still have trouble in understanding abstractions, but he will be eager

to eliminate that which is logically or morally unacceptable. As we will discuss at length, the more we explain
the intangible force called God *in terms of his own experiences,* the more real and conceivable God will be
to him.

As the youngster approaches his early teen-age years,
he begins to think critically and will be drawn to reject
many of his childish ideas. We should certainly encourage
him, making religion stand in his mind for the *duty* to
question and scrutinize, rather than making it an area too
sacred and too fragile to bear examination. We can now
replace childish ideas and compromises of language with
mature ideas which an adolescent should be prepared to
understand.

In trying to convey such an idea of God to young children, we are helped by what Piaget calls the functional
orientation of the child's mind. When a child asks what a
thing is, he is really asking what it does, what it is *for.*
He is not interested in a philosophical, conceptual definition. When he asks, "What is a chair?" he is looking for
the answer, "A chair is for sitting on," not "a chair is a
piece of furniture with four legs, a back and a flat area
above the legs." We would do well to remember that
when he asks about God he wants to be told what God
does, what difference God makes in his own life. Philosophical considerations about the nature of God, which
don't crop up in his living experience, could not interest
him less. This pattern of childhood thinking fits in very
well with our own way of comprehending God, that is to
say, in terms of what He makes possible in our lives rather

than in speculation as to what He is.

Again, child psychologists (mostly Piaget, who has done such monumental work in this area) tell us that the mind of the young child wants a neatly-ordered universe in which everything has its place. (This tendency presumably has nothing to do with the condition in which he leaves his rooms after playing.) A child believes everything that exists was made *by* someone *for* some purpose. He cannot believe that things "just happen." Piaget, for example, was once stumped by a child who asked him, "Why doesn't Lake Geneve go as far as Berne?" To an adult mind, Lake Geneve stops where it does because that is where it is located and where it extends to and that's it. The child's question was finally answered by another, older child who explained, to the questioner's great satisfaction that, "Every city has its own lake." (A suggestion: Sometimes a child's question will become more intelligible, and his frame of reference in asking it clearer, if we let him ask it of another, slightly older child, and see how the latter answers. We must be prepared, however, to give our own answers without calling the older youngsters wrong.)

We will be able to use to advantage this tendency of the young to see purposiveness behind all that exists, but it will also cause problems. There *are* things which "just happen" and we will have to find the time and place to communicate this to our children.

The "Jewish Santa Claus" issue, that is, the problem of teaching children things which we do not believe as true, because they are only children and the stories are enjoy-

able ones which are found in our tradition, is a serious
matter, and one for which I have no "Yes-or-No" answers. I can only offer the following guidelines:

(1) We must certainly share the traditional Bible
stories with our children. To do otherwise, out of religious
scruples, would be to deprive them of one of the most
precious, profound and fundamental aspects of their heritage. These stories have survived and been cherished by
more than a hundred generations because they say something to which the human spirit has responded. The
details are mythological, or embroidered by well-meaning
imagination, but underlying ideas of the stories have
struck responsive chords in the human soul. Like foods
that contain essential vitamins not yet isolated by science,
I believe the Hebrew (like the Greek and Norse) legends
nourish us at a level not easily translated into intellectual
terms.

What is more, children need drama and vicarious
excitement in their lives and they need heroes to emulate.
I would certainly want them to grow up in the company
of Jewish Biblical heroes and models, heroes of faith and
persistence, as well as with the muscular, pagan heroes of
Greek mythology and American television.

(2) The Bible tales we read them should be, for the
most part, "unexpurgated." I have never appreciated the
versions of "Red Riding Hood" or the "Three Little Pigs"
in which the wolf was turned into a harmless vegetarian
to spare the feelings of sensitive little listeners. I have
very little confidence in the abilty of the contemporary
parent to improve on the narratives of Genesis. The

stories in the Bible speak in the accents of another age, but they are works of genius. We should read them as they stand and explain them where and when necessary, pointing out that they were written long ago by people who saw the world differently than we do, rather than tamper with them.

(3) Children commute effortlessly between the real world and the world of their imagination. They learn rapidly enough that the monsters and magical figures of the storybook and television cartoons belong to a world apart from the one they and their famlies inhabit. We should keep the supernatural God in the storybook and not raise questions until our children do. There is absolutely no need for us to draw a moral for the child's own life based on a God who sees, hears, and punishes. The child himself will most likely put such a God in the same category as the wizards, talking animals, and magic beans of his other stories.

The following story, purportedly a true one, comforts us with the hope that the problem is less critical than we think. A precocious five-year-old girl had heard the legend that, at midnight on the eve of *Shavuot*, the festival of the giving of the *Torah*, the heavens open and one can see God on His throne. She begged and pleaded and cajoled for the right to stay up until midnight so she could see God. As persistent as her parents were in saying no, so was she in her demand. Finally, her mother said, "Look, you're only five and you can't stay up until midnight. But we'll compromise. Wait until you are ten and we'll let you do it then." Tearfully the girl replied, "But when I'm ten, I won't believe it any more."

Most children will outgrow these childish notions without much pain; we have to give them something to grow into. Should they turn to us for confirmation of their excessively literal ideas about God before they are ready to understand our more subtle and abstract answers, we can answer, "Well, yes, it's something like that but not exactly." Should they ask skeptical questions, we ought to look for an answer which will not detract from the dignity of the stories nor cause the children to scorn them. But we should not "plant weeds" by actually endorsing ideas which our children will later come to reject. We can say, "Many years ago, when people wanted to teach a very important lesson, (e.g. that cruel societies end up by destroying themselves or that people who are impatient and can't wait for something to happen in its own time often spoil everything) they told this story to make their point in a way audiences would enjoy hearing and would remember afterwards."

The problem of Santa Claus is not the trauma of the child's discovering that he doesn't exist, but the *absence of anything to replace him.* Learning that the man with the beard and red suit is imaginary does not hurt a child —it is learning that one's bountiful, dream-fulfilling, toy-dispensing world is imaginary that hurts. If we read our children anthropomorphic, highly-magical Bible stories without preaching concepts beyond the pages of the book, without invoking examples of divine intervention to reward and punish in the child's own life, without encouraging prayer to change the course of external events beyond our control . . . and if we, in addition, have suitable answers for the child who begins to probe and question the stories we read him, the problem may be no problem at all. If we do not encourage the child to believe that the wonderful, no-loose-ends world of the storybook is identical with his world, we may escape the trauma of his discovering that things don't happen in his life the way they do in the lives of the Biblical patriarchs.

We can't expect our children of pre-school and elementary-school age to be accomplished theologians, though the range of their interests and the subtlety of their minds often surprises us. But we can at least make sure that, when they begin to question the ideas about God to which their young minds naturally gravitate, they won't feel that they are betraying us or abandoning God or Judaism entirely. *If we teach them nothing else during their earliest years, we should be sure to teach them that the idea of God is a difficult one even for adults to understand, that our conception of it keeps on changing as we grow older and understand more and that our primary religious duty is to search, to question, to evaluate, and to try to comprehend.*

Chapter III

CHILDREN ASK ABOUT GOD

IN TRYING TO ANSWER a young child's questions, to his satisfaction as well as our own, there is no substitute for knowing at the outset *what* question he is really asking and what information he is seeking. Otherwise, we are liable to answer the question in our minds rather than in his. There is a classic story of the mother whose eight-year-old son came in from playing one day and asked: "Mommy, where did I come from?" The mother said to herself, "This is it," and sat him down to explain the whole process of reproduction and birth, complete with diagrams and pictures of the embryo at various stages of its development. When she finished, her son said, "That's all very interesting, but Jimmy comes from New Jersey; where did I come from?"

Let us keep in mind that Piaget found children's questions to be functional rather than theoretical and that the answers they want are those which will have meaning for their personal lives. For example, when a child asks, "Why is the grass green?", he is not interested in being told about chlorophyll or being given a "scientific explanation." He wants to be told something along the lines of, "so that the world will be all bright and pretty for you to look at." (Incidentally, there is nothing dishonest about such an answer. The human eye and nervous system are constructed in such a way that they find blue and green the most pleasant and relaxing colors.) The difference between the two possible answers is not that one is factual while the other is fanciful, but that one understands "Why?" to mean "from what cause?" and the other takes it, as children take it, to mean "for what purpose?" (This example also brings to mind the "unscientific" but charming line in the opening chapter of the Bible, where God is portrayed as setting the moon and the stars in the sky so that people will be able to keep track of the months and seasons, and know when the holidays fall.)

I can attest to the validity of Piaget's insight from personal experience. Whenever my five-year-old son watched the news on television with me, he would ask why the people were fighting in Vietnam and I would give him a "correct" social-political answer. It was a perfectly fine and accurate answer as far as I was concerned, but he kept asking me the same question over and over. Finally, with the help of Piaget, I realized that he wasn't really asking about the political interests in Vietnam. He wanted to know if *his* house would be bombed, *his* family and friends shot at, like the people on the TV screen. When I told him the fighting was very, very far away, that people were trying to stop it and that we didn't expect it to come anywhere near us, his anxiety lessened and the questions slacked off.

The moral of the story: It's a lot easier to answer a question when you understand precisely what the questioner is asking and why he is asking it.

"How Do I Know There Really Is a God?"

When a child asks this question, I wonder what he really has on his mind. I can't believe it is merely precocious theological-philosophical query. There may indeed be some curiosity about a mysterious, important subject, conversation about which he has overheard among adults. But basically, the question stems from some deeply-felt personal concern. And though it may be asked in the same words, it means different things to different children at different stages of their development. My own experience has led me to suspect that when a young child asks, "Is there really a God?" he is really concerned about a stable, secure, purposeful world. He wants to know if he can trust the world. When an older child, a pre-teen or teen-ager, asks the question, he is most likely concerned about the firmness of standards of right and wrong, justice and unfairness, in the world.

We must realize the world is a frightening place to a young child. It is huge, scaled beyond his size, filled with things too high for him to reach or too heavy for him to carry. It seems confusing and arbitrary, with so very many things happening at once, with rewards bestowed and punishments inflicted according to no discernible pattern. It is so uncontrollable—a world whose inhabitants are always making him do things without his being able to control or compel them in return. *If the idea of God is to mean anything to a young child, it ought to be reassuring.* It ought to do for him what belief in God did for the child who wrote this letter, included in the little volume *More Children's Letters to God* (compiled by

Eric Marshall and Stuart Hample, published by Simon and Schuster, New York):

"Dear God, Sometimes I am very scared in my room at night. I know you are there to protect me. Your friend, Diane."

Believing in God ought to convey the comforting knowledge that the world is a friendly, manageable place, that there is symmetry and coherence to it. We answer a child's question by communicating our own conviction that we can trust the world, that while disappointing and even tragic things sometimes happen, the world fundamentally makes sense. (This, of course, assumes that our own religious faith is itself grounded in that conviction.)

The young child's view of the world has been termed a "morality of security." That is, what makes him feel secure is valid, good and true. What lessens his security is "unacceptable" and is either evil or unreal. Here, the child re-enacts the first stage of man's religious growth and sees the world (and the gods of the world) as existing to meet his needs.

Probably the most important theological contribution we can make to our children at this point is to let them learn to trust *us*. If one's idea of God is inextricably intertwined with one's sense of authority and one is a belittling or punitive parent or teacher, your children will have difficulty believing in a God who is fair and loving.

Is there *really* a God? If we recognize God in our own power to grow and we do grow, becoming bigger and stronger, smarter and more skillful with the passage of time, this indicates that there is, indeed a God. If God's handiwork is seen in the vastly complex, orderly world, a world too intricately put together and too closely geared to human needs and fulfilment to be an accident, a world of unchanging laws which we can learn to understand and control, then the world seems to say to us that God shapes it. We find His fingerprints in the intricate orderliness of sunrise and sunset, in the changing seasons and cycles of weather. A child who has seen a flower grow from a seed can be taught to see God in the marvelous ways the smallest plants and animals are cared for.

(Teaching the reality of God through seasons and weather has its pitfalls, of course. "Why did God make it rain and spoil our picnic?" We must explain that we don't believe God decides every day where it will rain and where it will be sunny. He couldn't do it on the basis of what would make people happy, because there would always be some people who wanted or needed rain or snow while others wanted or needed sunshine and clear skies. Besides, that isn't how God operates. He saw to it that the world was made in such a way that the clouds give rain and that water and sunshine together make trees and plants and flowers and food grow. If He hadn't made the world that way, it would have been impossible for us or anything else to live in it.)

If we understand God to mean the Power that makes us feel in certain ways, the Spirit that causes us to know what Love and Hope and Compassion are like at all those moments when our spirits are in tune with the spirit of the universe, then we *can* believe that God is real—because we know that Love and Hope and Compassion are

real. We have felt them, we have been stirred by them
and they point to the reality of God.

Rabbi Ira Eisenstein has put it about as well as anyone:

> "Nobody ever saw electricity. We know that it
> exists. We can see and feel what electricity does.
> If we have an electric bulb and connect it with
> an electric wire, we get light. If we have an
> electric heater and connect it, we get heat . . .
> In other words, we get to know what electricity
> is by *what it does.* In the same way, we get to
> know what God is by what God makes us do.
> When a person is, so to speak, connected with
> God, he does good things . . . Whenever this
> force is active we say that God has exercised
> influence and power. (I. Eisenstein, *What We
> Mean by Religion.*)

We never come to know what God *is,* but we can become quite familiar with what God *does* and the reality
of this in our world points to the reality of the God Who
makes it possible. I have often asked a child, "Can you
think of something which is real but you can't see it or
touch it?" Almost invariably, the first answer will be
"the wind." That's a good answer; you can't see wind,
but you can feel its power and see it move things. The
next answer is usually "ideas, feelings, love, anger, fear."
You cannot see them. But you can see how people look
when they are angry or afraid, and you can feel these
feelings in yourself, so you know they are real. God, I
suggest, is real in that way. This is all we ever know about

God and fortunately, it is with this that children are most concerned.

How do we know there *is* a God? We reassure ourselves that God is real because He makes things happen and because He moves and inspires people, even as He has moved us at times to be more generous, more helpful, more patient than we might otherwise have been inclined to be. There were times when we were angry with someone and found it possible to forgive. There were times when we were lazy or afraid to try something new and we found the will and courage to go ahead. There were times when we were confused and then suddenly we knew what the right thing to do was. In these instances, God acted on us and made us different.

Let us be as vivid and concrete as we can in trying to establish the reality of an unseeable, intangible God. We cannot see or feel God Himself, but we *can* see and feel God-in-action. When you realize that you are bigger, stronger, smarter than you were a year ago, when you see a seed grow into a flower, when the sunshine makes the grass sparkle and the world looks beautiful, when you build something and it works, when people love you not for what you have done but just for being you, you know that God is the force in the world that makes it possible for all this to happen and that He makes life worthwhile.

For a Jewish child, the historical life of the Jewish people offers many examples of the abstraction we call God becoming real in people's lives. We ourselves have lived only a short time and not that much has happened to us. But the Jewish people has been in existence for more than 3,000 years and its history is rich in concrete illustrations of the reality of God. In the beginning of the Jewish story, a band of slaves in Egypt burst forth into freedom. In the first flush of their new-found freedom, they dedicated themselves to living a distinctive, consecrated way of life. The opening pages of Jewish history affirm that God's design for mankind calls for human beings to be free, not slaves and that liberation from restriction and oppression is possible in this world. They speak of responsibility and commitment as being the companion virtues of freedom.

The people of Israel went on to establish a nation which was never a great economic or military power, but went on to leave more of a mark on the world through its spiritual genius that did the great empires of the time. The Israelite way of life taught men how to find true greatness in small things and true divinity in the perfection of the soul and the civilization of the art of living. *"Not by might and not by power, but by My spirit, saith the Lords of Hosts."* (Zech. 14:6)

The greater part of Jewish history saw the people of Israel living in exile, often as a persecuted minority. The study of those centuries bears witness to Man's capacity to endure tragedy without having his faith shattered, his ability to be treated meanly without being driven to respond with meanness. For much of this period, the Jewish community existed in a context of brutality, venality and illiteracy, but it continued to stand for compassion, generosity and learning and in the process produced many remarkable people. While the teaching of Jewish history—with emphasis on our being persecuted—leads to problems and may make it difficult for a youngster to identify readily with a passive, suffering people, we should teach him that there is heroism in our ancestors' having stood up to brutalization without becoming brutalized themselves; we should show him that in their persistent attachment to God's values and God's ways, the Jews found God real in their lives. How else, if not by evoking God, can we explain their courage and dedication?

In our time, too, the Jewish people survived the trauma of the Holocaust and emerged from it still believing in the world's possibilities; thus we were able to establish and maintain the state of Israel in the face of obstacles that should have made it impossible.

Is God real? Philosophy can teach us only that God is plausible. But Jewish history shows us God in action—the freeing of the slaves, their decision to commit themselves to the *Torah,* the guidance in their building of a small, weak people into a nation which changed the face of the world, their strength in enduring tragedy and resisting brutalization and the faith and the energy involved in building Israel in the years following the Second World War. We experience the reality of God in our own lives, but we experience it vicariously as well when we examine the history of the Jewish people. No one who reads the story of our 3,000 years of tribulation and accomplishment can deny that God makes a difference in the world.

"Does God Know Everything I Do?"

We have said that if the belief in God is to mean anything to a young child, it must be reassuring. It must say to him, and plausibly, that this is an essentially friendly, intelligible, livable world. Yet have we ever stopped to consider how unsettling, even frightening, the traditional idea of God is to a youngster? What does it do to a child when he is taught that God is invisible, that He is everywhere and knows everything we do? Could anything be more perfectly calculated to produce fear and guilt? We tend to forget how incredibly vulnerable the egos of young children (and most adults) are to feelings of guilt and shame, how easily their souls can be warped by the careless suggestion that they are inadequate or no good. Children are only too ready to accept verdicts of others that they do not measure up. They live on a threshold of dread that their secret, shameful thoughts about their parents, family and selves—and the forbidden deeds of their fantasy lives—will be discovered.

One ten-year-old boy I know was very upset when he learned he would need glasses. No one could understand why. Finally, the story came out. Shortly before a routine eye examination, this boy and a few older friends were looking through a neighbor's trash set out for collection and had found a copy of *Playboy* magazine. When he was told a week later that he needed glasses, the boy literally believed that God was striking him blind for looking at naughty pictures. Teaching children that God sees everything they do may introduce elements of fear and guilt into a normal young mind.

There may have been a time when religion was based on "the fear of the Lord" (the Biblical term, by the way, means more nearly "awe," "reverence" at the thought of His greatness, not fright; the "fire and brimstone" orientation was a later development and for most part a non-Jewish one.) But we certainly regard that as obsolete today. We don't want our children to obey us because they are afraid of us, or because they are afraid of being discovered and punished. We want them to heed us because they have come to understand that what we stand for is right and because they have learned to trust and respect our judgment and fairness, even when our reasons for demanding something are not totally clear. To obey us out of fear is to feel free to disobey us as soon as they are old enough or far enough from home not to be afraid of us any more. So it is in the ideas of God they have. Obedience to God based on the fear that He knows everything and punishes sinners all too soon becomes a religion that offers no plausible objection to wrong-doing to the skeptical mind which can no longer believe in such a God, or has learned from experience and observation that God's punishments are far from reliable.

By all means, let us teach our children that what they think and do counts, that it helps to shape their character. Let us never teach them to feel themselves depraved and unworthy because they are less skilled than most adults in repressing unpleasant, unacceptable thoughts and forcing them underground. Let them know that every person, even the finest and most decent of men, has such thoughts and that in good people they remain only fantasies, temptations which we put aside. And certainly let us teach them to believe in a God who helps them become strong enough to sift through their thoughts and resist the bad ones, rather than to believe in a God who snoops, reads minds, and condemns to death.

Similarly the idea that God is omniscient and knows everything that happens and is going to happen, is an attempt, I am sure, to express the greatness and all-inclusiveness of God, but it ends up only confusing the issue. It raises the immensely complex problem of Free Will vs. Predestination: "If God knew what I was going to do, then I was predestined to do it; I had no choice but to do it and therefore I shouldn't be held responsible for what I did." What is more, to claim God knows everything elicits from the average child not the awe and admiration it is supposed to, but a "wise guy" resentment and the wish to take God down a peg or two. In the thoroughly charming collection, *Children's Letters to God,* we find the following communications:

"Dear God, If you are so smart, let's see if you can read what I am saying. It's in my own code, and no one knows it: VDDL RBT CLJKS NT PSD KLHSM ATFO. (If you can read it, make it rain tomorrow so I will know.) Your unknown friend, Gabe."

"Dear God, Can you guess what is the biggest river of all of them? You ought to be able to, because you made it. Ha Ha. Guess who."

Whoever invented the fancy Greek-and-Latin word "omniscient" (all-knowing) and attached it to God in an attempt to flatter or magnify Him or to be logically consistent with statements about His unlimited powers, did Him no favor. I don't believe that "God *knows* everything." I think the very question inevitably bogs us down in the morass of discussing God in human terms and applying the results to our understanding of religion and the world.

First of all, I don't believe that God "knows" by means of the same mental processes that you and I "know" things. And if He "knows" things by a different process, which human beings can't comprehend, I see very little point in discussing problems raised by His "knowing." This is another one of the problems raised, not by life experiences, but by our habit of using human terms of reference in talking about God. To speak of "God's knowing" or "God's remembering" cannot mean that God has a brain or a mind like some kind of human quiz champion.

Moreover and more importantly, I simply cannot accept the notion that God "knows the future" before it happens. The concepts of human freedom of action and human responsibility for its actions are too basic to my view of life, and to Judaism in general, for me to give them away in the interest of a Greek-and-Latin word game. (Admittedly, classical Jewish thinkers were reluctant to deny God any power or ability, but at the same time they refused to diminish Man's freedom or his responsibility for what he does. Typical was Rabbi Akiba's answer, which tried to maintain both at the price of paradoxality or the loss of logical consistency: *"Every-*

thing is foreseen but we have freedom of decision.")

For the same reason, I remain skeptical of people's premonitions of airplane crashes or, for instance, of the assassination of President Kennedy, premonitions which tend to be remembered only when they "come true" and are usually made public after the event. I believe that these events were free not to happen, had people at the last moment chosen to act differently and that they could not have been foreseen. The future does not exist, like the next reel of a movie, while we wait for it to happen to us. We shape the future and it has no shape or content until we provide them.

God is not all-knowing in the sense of anticipating all of our decisions before we ourselves have decided upon them. A God who sees and knows everything would arouse feelings of guilt, self-consciousness and apathy among His followers. A God who stands for unlimited possibilities, who can help us to do those fulfilling things which we decide to try to do, who won't do things to us, but will make it possible for us to do things for ourselves —such a God liberates us and helps us grow. We *are* free to decide for ourselves what we want to do and what sort of people we want to be. Let's not permit the imprecise use of theological language or the desire to "credit" God with all sorts of amazing powers keep us from recognizing this.

Should we try to soften the impact of an all-seeing, all-knowing God by teaching that He does indeed know all our good and bad deeds and thoughts, but that He is merciful and forgiving, we won't do much better. (This

includes the variation that God will forgive us if we
repent, or that He will forgive us if we ask Him nicely
enough and bring Him presents. I believe in *Teshuva,*
Repentance, but I don't think it is a matter of telling God
we're sorry and His answering "All right, but don't let
it happen again.") A theology which teaches us that God
is aware of our wrongdoings but is willing to forgive and
put up with the likes of us, is really teaching the weakness
of Man. It implies that Man is unreliable and never adds
up to very much, except insofar as God is willing to take
pity on so imperfect a creature and accept him as he is.
This is something one hears often enough from many
pulpits; I find it both factually and psychologically
wrong.

There is a very important difference between teaching,
on the one hand, that Man is so given to making mistakes
that he can never straighten himself out and so must depend on God to accept him as he is and teaching, on
the other hand, that the same man who makes mistakes
is also capable of recognizing and correcting his mistakes,
if he chooses to use some of the qualities God has given
him. It is not so much a matter of God's "knowing" our
shortcomings and putting up with us; rather, it is Man
who must know his own shortcomings and call on the
Spirit we call God to give him the ability to improve and
the vision to see his abilities and defects realistically.

Man is not hopeless and unworthy and for the most
part knows it. He may not be everything he ought to be
and may not be everything he would like to be. He is
certainly not everything he might be. All the same, he has

done some marvelous things in the world of science and technology, in the healing arts and he has been responsible for some impressive works of creativity and compassion. We know enough about how the human soul works to realize that even if a person is grossly imperfect, we don't improve him by constantly harping on his unworthiness and reminding him how fortunate he is that we are willing to put up with him. We would certainly not appreciate that sort of attitude from our friends or co-workers. We should not treat our children that way as parents, nagging them about their mistakes and wondering aloud how much longer we will be able to stand them. Why then should anyone say God is like that, keeping track of every little thing we do wrong, and putting up with us for His mercy's sake if not for ours? I would rather our children think of God in terms of *what they can do with Him and because of Him,* if they let Him help them, rather than in terms of *what He can do to them* if they disobey His will or try to hide from His "all-seeing eye."

Let us tell our children that there isn't a God-person in Heaven keeping track of what you do, but let them know that everything we do *does* count and cannot be ignored or disregarded. If you sometimes do wrong, it becomes harder not to do it the next time. Soon it may become a habit and it will be even harder to keep it from becoming a permanent part of you. Every deed, good or bad, leaves its mark on our character, even if it is not literally recorded in a "heavenly book."

To believe that "Man was made in the image of God"

certainly doesn't mean that we look like God physically. He has no physical form for us to resemble. What it means is that there is a little bit of God, of that Spirit which makes the world a certain kind of place, in every one of us. Some people call it our soul or our conscience, just as the Power we call God can be thought of as the Soul or Conscience of the universe. Like God, this Soul or Conscience is not a thing, a bone or muscle located somewhere in our body, which we can find and touch and measure. It is a collection of feelings and attitudes we are capable of having. A soul is what makes a human being different from an animal, a living person different from a dead one and a good, kind, sensitive person different from a mean, selfish one. Every human being has a soul. (We keep talking about it as though it were a thing, though we must remember that it isn't. We don't "have" a soul; we *are* a soul. The word is really better understood as an adjective, a quality of relationship, than as a noun—even as "God" is more accurately used as an adjective than as a noun. We know "godly deeds," "godly behavior," "divinely inspired action" a lot more clearly than we know God Himself.)

A soul is what makes it possible for a man to be in tune with the Power we call God and to be potentially capable of growing into a remarkably fine, helpful, creative person. Every single human being is potentially a spiritual masterpiece. It is this belief about God and about the godliness in each of us, that lets us have faith in ourselves, even when we've let ourselves down by doing things that were wrong, that lets us keep faith in the future of the human race, even when it disappoints our expectations.

"Why Can't I See God? Is He Invisible?"

The concept of an invisible, all-seeing God is not only hard for an adult to take seriously, it is psychologically harmful and counter-productive. It frightens, when belief in God ought to reassure. It invokes guilt and furtiveness instead of confidence and trust. What, then, do we put in its place?

First, we should neither believe personally nor communicate to our children the idea that God is *invisible*. "Invisible" implies that God has form and shape, but that we are not capable of seeing Him.

God is *intangible:* we can't see Him because there is nothing there to be seen. He is one of those forces which are real though they have no shape and don't take up space. Like love, joy, healing, hot and cold, we can "see" God only through the difference He makes in the people and things of the world. We can't see or touch love or joy; we *can* see and touch people whose lives are changed by love and joy.

Similarly the idea that God is everywhere at once is a misleading, and perhaps a meaningless one. If God is equally distributed through the world, then for all practical purposes, He is nowhere. That is, He is nowhere more than anywhere else and has no real existence. Besides, the statement that "God is everywhere" has given rise to more ludicrous misunderstandings in the minds of children than perhaps any other theological proposition ever uttered. Children have been quoted as saying, in fear or in glee, that God was in the bathtub, in the dark closet, in their sandwich; the solemnity and dignity of the Divine seem to have gotten lost in the process.

I might suggest that, instead of talking about "where is God?" we rephrase the question and ask "when is God?" "Where is God?" would seem to imply that God is a thing, an object taking up space, whose location, or several simultaneous locations, can be pinpointed, like the deity the Russian cosmonaut thought he might bump into, were he to be in the right place at the right instant. To ask "when is God?" suggests that God is not an object, but a quality of relationship, a way of feeling and acting, that can be found anywhere, but only if certain things (study, gratitude, self-control, helpfulness, prayer, etc.) are in evidence at that particular moment. God is certain things happening; He is the awareness that the world is constructed so as to encourage these things to happen. Asking "when is God?" solves part of the problem of children who want to know why they have to go to services at set times and why "God can't hear them" when they pray at home. We go to services on Friday evenings and Saturday mornings not because God keeps "office hours" then, not because God is imprisoned in our local sanctuary waiting for us to visit Him there, but because Jews coming together for worship can summon up a feeling of godliness, a feeling of the presence of God in their midst and together can fashion a moment when they can feel His reality more clearly than any one of them would be able to by himself.

Where, then, is God? He is not everywhere. He is potentially anywhere; when people act and treat each other in certain ways, so that the Spirit of God flows between them, we can say that God is then present.

"Can I Be Absolutely Sure That There Is a God?"

Children who have absorbed something of the scientific method and children for whom the existence of a benign providence is very important, are likely to probe beyond our statements about the reality of God and ask if they can be *absolutely sure* that He exists. This is only partly a question about God. It is also partly a question about the quality of their own belief and the reliability of the world. Children often find it difficult to be tentative about things that are important to them.

Can we be sure that the sort of God we have been talking about is real and not a figment of our imagination or a result of wishful thinking? There are few enough things about which we can be absolutely sure. Even a scientist can't be absolutely sure about the physical laws with which he works. All he can say is that "they seem to fit what we know about a subject, lead to the results we anticipate when we employ them and there is no evidence to contradict them. For that reason, I assume they are true and I will go on using the assumption. If evidence ever turns up to prove they are not true, then I will stop believing and using them and will try to formulate a new set of rules which will make sense of that new evidence."

There was a time when people made a distinction between Faith and Knowledge. Knowledge was what you knew for an absolute certainty to be true; Faith was what you accepted as true even in the absence of definitive proof. The trouble was that what was called Knowledge turned out to be a lot less certain than people thought it was; there was an element of faith in assuming that a "working hypothesis" which one held until proven wrong was indeed valid. What was called Faith all too often included things which were not only unproven and un-provable, but demonstrably false.

What does it mean, "to be sure that there is a God?" Again, it is not really a question about the population of Heaven. To believe that God is real means believing that the qualities we associate with God are real, that they truly exist in the world. If we have experienced love, trust, generosity, either as donors or as recipients, if we have known the feeling of being honest or helpful, then we know from our own experience, not based on anyone else's philosophy or persuasiveness, that these qualities are real beyond all question. If we have felt the striv-ings of goodness in ourselves, this is evidence of the reality of God in our own hearts. And if we understand "God" to mean the Power that makes these experiences possible, the reality of these experiences should bear eloquent witness to the reality of God. We cannot prove or disprove whether there is an old man with a long beard dwelling in Heaven, but we can definitely prove that God, the Source of growth, love and truth, does exist.

Rabbi Henry Cohen has written a beautiful testament to the reality of God which will help the child sustain his belief in His reality:

"God will be with you as you grow physically from a child to a man (or woman), for God is the Power that makes for growth.

"God will be with you as you grow emotionally, from an infant who thinks primarily of his own pleasure, to a truly human being who somehow comes to care about the needs of others,, for God is the Power that makes for love.

"God will be with you as your own mind grows in wisdom, as you come to understand more about yourself and your world, for God is the Power that makes for the clear use of reason.

"God will be with you when, after days of anxiety and confusion, the dawn breaks and suddenly you see where you are going, for God is the Power that makes for a better tomorrow." (Reconstructionist, Vol. 23, #9, June, 23, 1967).

We can't prove beyond the shadow of a doubt that God is real, but as our own life-experiences convince us that growth is real and reliable, that love is real and not imaginary, that our abilities to think and to will are real, we can become ever more confident that our belief in the reality of a God who stands for these things is well-founded.

"Do I Have to Believe in God to Be Good?"

What do we mean by the phrase "to believe in God?" It means, first of all, believing in yourself, believing that you have the capacity to grow and become a good person.

It means believing that you *ought* to become a good person, as good as you are capable of being, that this is somehow an obligation of anyone who is alive and human.

"To believe in God" means, too, to believe in goodness, to believe that certain things are right and worth doing even if they are hard, and other things are wrong and should not be done, no matter how tempting they may be. Belief in God, as we understand it, is a basis for taking life seriously and taking human behavior seriously.

Good people may be good for any number of reasons —fear, self-interest, commitment to an ideal, social pressure. The person who is good because he believes that certain things are right and because he wants to be a person who does what is right is being good out of a belief in God. He need not take literally the image of a divine person in Heaven observing and marking down his deeds, but he believes in God and is acting on that belief.

God as Father

A number of prayers and other references speak of God as "Father," which is a very concrete, highly emotional image. How are we to understand them? A father is a real, live person who cares about us, talks to us and listens to us and gives us what we want and need. The word, as used by children, may refer not only to their real-life father, but to an idealized, perfect Father as they would like to have him and it is this latter sense that they often understand the word when applied to God. Throughout history, people have chosen to believe that God was a father in the above mentioned sense, because they wanted to believe that the world would give them what they wanted and would protect them from danger. It might be very reassuring today to believe that we have a "Father in Heaven" treating us as an ideal, all-powerful parent would; unfortunately, there is too much evidence against such a belief.

In addition, Rabbi Roland Gittelson has noted that thinking of God as "Father" invites the projection of all of a child's conscious and unconscious resentments toward his father onto his image of God. Rabbi Gittelson suggests that we de-personalize the idea of God as Father and substitute the parallel but less emotionally laden idea of God as Source.

Where texts refer to God as Father, we understand them to mean that God is the Source of life, the Power that makes it possible for us and for other living things to be alive. He is the Source of wisdom and knowledge and of the ideals for which we live, not because He is a Superperson giving us things as a generous father might, but because the word "God" stands for the existence of wisdom, knowledge, and other ideals in the world. In this way, we keep the valid insights contained in the image of God as Father, without introducing the distracting notions of personality, concreteness or resentment.

"Who Made God?"

The question "who made God?" seems to be a perennial favorite of budding young theologians, each of whom thinks he is the first to have discovered it. It is a natural one for the young child to ask, because every child instinctively assumes that everything in the world was made *by* someone *for* some purpose. And it is a difficult question for the parent to answer, because it calls on us to use common, ordinary words with very different meanings from the ones they usually have. This is hard enough for us to do and harder for a young child to comprehend.

At such times, in dealing with this question and with several others, we can use an approach on which Dr. Sophia Fahs has written, and say to our young children: "That's a very good question. When I hear you ask it, I realize how grown up you are becoming because you are starting to think about things that grown-ups think about. That is a question grown-ups have been thinking about for a long time. We don't have the whole answer, but we have something we can say about it, and what you don't understand today, you may understand a little better when you're still older than you are now. Who knows, you may even come up with answers to it that no one has ever thought of before, as you continue to try to understand it."

We might then go on to say: God isn't a person, or a thing, or an object. He is a Force or Spirit. God means being inspired to do certain things, feeling certain ways, the deeds and the feelings that our religion speaks of as being god-like, the deeds and feelings that make us good people. This means that nobody really "made God," because He wasn't made or created the way a thing or a person is. When there was no world or anything, God wasn't anywhere, because there wasn't any place in the world for Him to be. Then the world came into being, a long, long time ago (and nobody knows how that happened, because it happened long before there were any people in the world, although later they used to tell stories about how they thought it all started) and certain things started happening in this world... the things we associate with God. And then God came into the world.

Later on, when there were people in the world and they could do so many things that animals and plants couldn't do—loving and creating and laughing and crying and building machines and writing poems and painting pictures—God was even more in the world. God became real and important in the world when these particular things began to happen in it.

"But I thought God created the world, and you say it came into being?"

He did create it, but not in the same way a carpenter makes a chair or a shoemaker a pair of shoes. He didn't put it together and shape it. The world was shaped by forces and events that took place a long time ago, so long ago—at a time when there weren't any people around to see and describe it—that nobody is sure just how it happened. But when we say that "God made the world," we mean that it turned out to be a certain kind of world, a world in which certain very important things can happen because God is a part of it. God made it become a world in which these things could happen and when they started to happen, then God became a real and important part of it.

"Does that mean that if nobody in the whole world did any of those good things, there would be no God?"

If nobody in the whole world did anything which was good and godly, God would still be real, He would still be possible, but He wouldn't be anywhere in the world. He would only be a possibility. He would be like a student who knows his work but never answers any questions, or a person who had a certain ability but never used it. If *nobody* called on the Power we call God to help them do good things, it wouldn't make any difference to the world whether there really was a God or not. Men who do good things in this world don't *make* God, but they bring Him into the world and let Him make a difference to their lives.

"Does God Care About Me, or About What I Do?"

This is another hard question to answer without misleading or mystifying. God isn't a person up in the sky, watching us all day long, smiling or frowning, laughing or scolding. God doesn't have feelings, the way people do. But in a sense, what kind of person you are makes a difference to the world, more of a difference than you can imagine. The kind of person you decide to be can make God stronger and more important in the world. By being a good, honest, helpful person, you can make it easier for others to believe in God, because you make the world seem nicer to them. You make goodness and honesty more real in their lives as well as in your own. By being mean and selfish, you make it harder for others to believe there is a God in the world. They can't understand why, if God made the world, there is so much meanness in it. There is a little bit of godliness in you, and one of the most important things you can do for your own life and for the world you live in, is to strengthen that feeling of godliness, to help it grow.

In this connection, we should clarify what we mean by "the will of God." Clearly, we don't mean that we have received requests or demands from a Person in Heaven, whom we feel obliged to obey—though many people accept or reject religion in precisely these terms. If the term "God" refers to the existence of certain qualities in the cosmos and in ourselves, the "will of God" would mean those laws of Nature, both physical and spiritual nature, which govern our becoming real and fully developed human beings. Phrases such as "the will of God," "what God wants me to do," "what God demands of us" reflect the conclusions to which men have come as to how we should live. Respect for our health and safety, moderation in food and drink, telling the truth, cooperating with others, feeling compassion, studying, respecting the dignity and property of others—these are examples of "what God wants us to do," in the sense that they are the "ground rules" governing our efforts to grow and fulfill ourselves in a world in which God is a real and significant force. As we will discuss later, to ignore these demands, to "disobey the will of God" is to run the risk of frustrating ourselves in our quest for fulfillment.

"How Do I Know There Is a God?" *(asked by an older child)*

I have suggested that a young child who asks about the existence of God is really asking whether he can trust the world. When the same question is asked by an older child, pre-teen or teenager, I suspect its purpose is similar, but enriched and deepened by his greater experience and his new-found capacity for abstract thought. When the older child asks about God, I think he is really worried about whether the all-too obvious loose threads of the world can be tucked into an orderly pattern and (as his own capacity for shame grows into an abstract considera- tion of Right and Wrong) whether firm, reliable standards of right and wrong exist. Whereas the young child wants to know whether the world threatens *him* or is disposed well toward him, the older child wants to know whether it threatens people in general or treats them with fairness and consideration. "Is there a God?" means, at least in part: "Does all this apparent injustice and conflict make sense somehow? Is there Someone or Something to define what is Right and what is Wrong? Or does that whole immense burden fall on my young shoulders?"

Remember, if you will, our suggestion that the God-idea parallels in its evolution the individual's concept of authority and his relationship to it. From the time the child is old enough to understand the concepts of "per- mitted" and "forbidden" to the time of his struggle for autonomy in mid-adolescence, the child's morality is one of simple obedience. His parents, along with teachers, TV announcers, and other authority figures in his life, tell him what he should and should not do, and there is no question that "being a good boy" means nothing more or less than obedience to their standards and demands. Rarely, if ever, does "being a good boy" involve evaluating a situation on its own merits and deciding for oneself.

Like the religionists who rose above the paganism in which God was concerned only with giving them life and food, to reach a morality-centered faith in which God rewarded them for following His commandments, the child believes implicitly in the wisdom and justice of what his parents teach him and demand from him. "It is too! My father said so!" becomes a watchword in their conversation and the ultimate authority. Life in its myriad options and multiple choices becomes so much more manageable and so much less frightening when our parents are there to tell us what can be done and what should be avoided, to supply us with a map for threading our way through the maze.

In answering a child's question at this point, we have to affirm, first of all, the existence of Right and Wrong (assuming again, of course, that we ourselves believe this) without leading the youngster to believe too literally in a "Father in Heaven" who advises, supervises, rewards and punishes, the way earthly parents do. There can be Right, without an enforcer of Right. It is worth noting that children at this stage should now be capable of considerable sophistication in many areas and there should be no reason, beyond our own problems of communication, for them to continue picturing God as so many of them do—as a bearded Lawgiver and heavenly Record-Keeper. They should no longer be as uncomfortable, as they were when they were younger, with abstractions.

Is there really a God? Let us ask, "If there were, what difference would it make? How would the world be different? If there were a God, there would be a moral intelligence to the world. The world would make sense. Certain things would be Right, and other things would be Wrong, that is, contrary to the goals and purposes of human beings.

"If there really were a God, we would see examples of people around us devoting their lives to being honest, helpful, creative. We would see ordinary people discovering resources of courage and dedication they never knew they had within themselves. We would find ourselves and others responding to good deeds, acts of self-sacrifice or restraint, with a sense of satisfaction, of 'rightness,' which would be hard to describe but which we would nonetheless feel strongly. We would find ideals and serious purposes highly attractive and the goal of improving the world and leaving it a little better for our having lived in it a moving one. Now let us see how closely our world meets these requirements."

The question of absolute Right and Wrong means firstly, do such absolute standards exist, and secondly, do we know what they are?

We can't prove that certain things are Right (not just attractive to us) and others are Wrong (not just frowned upon by our culture), but we can make a fundamental commitment of faith to the probability and desirability of that idea. Young people tend to be great "liberals," convinced that "everybody can believe and act as he wants to, as long as he doesn't hurt anybody else," easily persuaded that because some societies practice polygamy or have different styles of dress or child-rearing, their way is as "right" for them as ours is for us.

While we may admire their magnanimity and open-mindedness, I would not want them to believe that all morality is relative, that if the Eskimoes believe in exchanging wives or starving their elderly parents, one has the right to say, "when in Nome, do as the Eskimoes do." And if the existence of God is linked to the existence of Right and Wrong, I think we have to challenge them on this view. I have found this approach to be effective with older children:

(1) Even if there are such things as Right and Wrong, it doesn't mean that everything is either absolutely right or totally wrong. There are many areas—culinary habits, clothing, etc.—in which morality doesn't apply. And in these areas, we can certainly say of other societies, "Their way is as right for them as ours is for us." Outside the realm of morals, questions of human purpose and of Right and Wrong, there is the realm of mores, customs a society observes without claiming absolute rightness for them, simply because they are the traditional ways of behaving in that society.

(2) But can't we imagine that the human soul, like the human body, is made in such a way, that certain things are good for it, things which fit in with the way it was made to operate, and that other things are bad for it? When it comes to our bodies, we know that certain things are true whether we are in favor of them or not. No society can decide by majority vote that cookies are more nourishing than vegetables. It just wouldn't work; people who tried to live by that decision would simply not be as

healthy as they would want to be. And no society can decide by majority vote that people should be able to go out in the rain without raincoats and not get sick, or jump off buildings without risking injury.

Why can't the human soul be understood as operating in the same way? There are things it needs to do, and things it needs to avoid, if it is to grow up to be strong and healthy. And religion, when it speaks to us of Right and Wrong, is trying to *share with us its discoveries and experiences* about what our spirits need in order to grow and thrive.

The late Professor Edmond Cahn, a brilliant and original philosopher of law and morals, once posited a principle which he called the "sense of injustice," that is, our apparently instinctive capacity to say in certain situations, "that's not fair." What we mean when we say this (and children say it so readily) is not only, "I don't like the idea, I find it unsatisfying," but, "it's wrong, it goes against some universal rule which everybody has to respect, whether he likes it or not!" Our instinctive readiness to label some things unfair and our agreement that others (for example, murder) are so self-evidently wrong that no society has the right to legalize them seems to reveal a built-in conviction that Right and Wrong are not entirely man-made concepts, but that they exist independently of our ratification or consent. Crying "unfair" is an emotional vote in favor of the existence of absolutes and "God" is the name we give to the fact that these absolute standards, in conformity with which our spirits flourish, do indeed exist in the world.

This, incidentally, is an important concept in Biblical morality and specifically in the Ten Commandments. Other, pre-Israelite societies also had laws forbidding theft, murder, and adultery, but they usually took this form: "If a man deliberately kills another man, then his punishment shall be..." The Bible put it differently: "You shall not murder!"

In other words, murder is not just against the law and punishable, like double-parking but more serious. It is an *absolute* wrong that does not require human ratification to make it wrong and is not subject to human veto.

(3) Saying that there are absolute rights and wrongs is not quite the same as saying that we know exactly what they are or that one religious tradition has a complete and exhaustive inventory of them. If God were really a Heavenly Father, communicating His will to us His children much as our parents and teachers do (and presumably doing a better job of it, being less susceptible to human foibles of wording and temperament), there would, theoretically, be no problem. God would find a way of telling us what we needed to know.

But if God is the spirit that makes a certain kind of human fulfillment possible, we come to "know His will" much more gradually and less clearly. We learn by trial-and-error methods of discovering what enhances human life and what restricts and distorts it. We learn through the sudden insights of prophets and geniuses, insights into the nature and destiny of the human soul, and from the verification that the passage of time and the scrutiny of passing generations has given these insights. Little by little, we find ourselves coming to know "what the Lord requires of us" as we struggle to become authentically human.

The foregoing raises the important question, perhaps not strictly part of our subject, of how to teach our children to respond to other people's different beliefs about God and the world. I believe the following guidelines to be helpful:

It goes without saying that we can believe wholeheartedly in the conclusions to which reason and tradition have led us and still recognize our neighbor's right to different conclusions. This is not to say, "It doesn't matter what a man believes, as long as he believes something." I think what he believes matters a great deal. Nor is it the condescending tolerance of the English vicar who supposedly said, "You worship God in your way and I'll worship Him in His." It is rather the recognition that, even if we are sure that we are right and our neighbor wrong, humility and decency give us no cause to act on that conviction.

What about our children's friends, Jewish and Christian (and atheist) who believe differently? It is difficult for us to realize how strongly young children want to be the the same as their friends and how unsettling it may be for them to have their differences stressed. Some of the beliefs of these friends, let me point out, are really very much like ours, though phrased in different words or using different forms. They have their customs and holidays and we have ours, which means not that one way is right and the other way wrong but that different families and different groups of families have their own ways of doing things. Some of their ideas are different but do not conflict with ours because they don't deal with the same subject. So they can believe as they do, and we can believe as we choose to believe: we are different but not in conflict. Where they do disagree irreconcilably, let us remember that the ultimate purpose of religion is not the same as that of science, which is to discover the truth. Religion is *concerned* with truth, but concerned with it as an intermediate step on the way to an ultimate end—the creation of the kind of person who will live up to the full potential of his humanity. In the same way that two people may require different medicines for the same illness, different people may respond to different religious regimens while pursuing the same ultimate goals.

When your youngster comes in and says, "Jimmy and his family believe that God punishes you for not going to services every week," or "Barbara told me that God makes people die because He needs them more in Heaven than we do down here," I don't think I'd say to him, "Well, maybe they're right." Nor would I say, "That's silly, they don't know what they're talking about." I would suggest that maybe they just use different words to say something similar to what we say and we misunderstand them slightly. Or else I would say that since the purpose of religion is to fashion good people, what they say also helps them become good. It may be something we ourselves can't accept and live with, but perhaps in its own way, their religion does for them what ours does for us. And we should be happy that Jimmy and Barbara

take their religion seriously, if it helps make them nice
people.

Does it surprise the reader that I am so little concerned
with the issue of religious truth? A religious idea can be
true in one of two ways. It can be *literally* true, in the
sense that it describes accurately a condition that actually
exists or a historical event that actually took place as
described. (Either the world was created in six days or it
wasn't; either Jesus walked on water or he didn't. Either
there is an afterlife in which the good are rewarded or
there isn't.) Or it can be *functionally* valid, in the sense
that it achieves the purpose of helping people to understand the world and live up to certain ideals in it. A great
many religious ideas, which can never be proven or dis-
proven, work in the latter fashion. My concern is not
with physical or historical accuracy; I am no more certain
that God lacks hands and feet than someone else is certain
He has them. Our answers to questions about God differ
from the answers of Orthodox Judaism, Christianity, and
Buddhism, not solely because we think their answers are
inaccurate (something which is not provable) but because
we don't believe that they "work." As hypotheses, they
do not command the intellectual respect of bright, in-
quiring children and even if accepted, they do not guide
our children to grow up with the view of the world and
themselves we'd like them to have.

Chapter IV

DON'T BLAME GOD FOR
"ACTS OF GOD"

THIS MAY WELL BE the most important chapter in my book. It is certainly the one I was most eager to write and it covers several difficult areas with which we need to deal. The place of God in questions of death and misfortune, His role as rewarder of virtue and punisher of wrongdoing, are among the most sensitive subjects we confront. They are rarely explained well and too often well-meaning explainers do more harm than good. Once again, the key to success lies in the clarification of the issues in the minds of parents so that they can give honest and helpful answers to their children.

Consider two incidents: firstly, a mother, watching her little girl in a playground, tells her not to run away from the immediate vicinity. The girl leaves, falls down, skins her knee, and begins to cry. Her mother says, "You see, God is punishing you for not listening to your mother!" Do we really believe—do we want our children to believe—in a God who has nothing better to do than trip little girls in playgrounds?

Secondly and more seriously, a woman in my congregation dies of leukemia, leaving a 15-year-old son. The boy's aunt, trying to comfort him, tells him, "God took your mother because He needed her in Heaven more than you did here." I am sure the aunt was trying to be helpful, but she could scarcely have given him a worse, more harmful answer. First of all, she described God as having "taken" the mother, as having made a *conscious decision* in this specific case to end a woman's life. It would seem inevitable for the bereaved child to resent God for having caused the tragedy and to think of Him as a heavenly kidnapper—*instead of being able to call upon the resources represented by God to cope with his loss.* To compound the damage, the aunt committed the theological and psychological atrocity of adding, "God needed her more than you did." In such circumstances, a person inevitably has guilt feelings. "If I had been a better person, this wouldn't have happened to me. I'm being punished for my bad deeds and bad thoughts. All the angry wishes I had against my mother came true and I'm getting what I deserve. It's all my fault!" To confirm this by saying, even by implication, "If you had needed (that is to say, loved, appreciated) your mother more, she would still be alive" is thoughtlessly cruel.

God as Punisher

As in so many of these difficult theological areas, we must begin by ridding ourselves of the habit of thinking of God as a Superperson. He is not a wise, powerful old man sitting in Heaven, doing what people do but doing it better than they and free of human fallibility. In our prayers, we may speak of Him as a Judge. On the High Holidays, we may describe Him as sitting in judgment and deciding the fate of man. But this is another example of poetic language which, taken literally, is dangerously misleading.

It is tempting for parents and for adults in general, to picture God as an all-wise, unerring distributor of reward and punishment. It would be nice to believe that the world was run that well. It is simple to invoke His judgment, as so many parents do, in order to insure that their own commands are obeyed, even when they are not around to enforce them. It is tempting for children, too, to believe in such a God, because their minds seem to gravitate instinctively toward orderliness, to an arrangement in which everything is in its place and there are no loose ends. It is fascinating to learn of the fantasies they concoct and of the intricate theories they invent in order to make the known facts of their world fit neatly together.

Ultimately, anyone who measures his theories against the inescapable realities of life will have to give up the neat view and acknowledge the fact that there is a certain amount of randomness in the world, a residue of chaos. There *are* things which happen for no discernible reason. Some—earthquakes and heart attacks—probably issue out of very specific natural causes which we haven't yet come to understand, predict or control. Others—which particular person happens to be in the path of a drunkard's car or a maniac's bullet—will probably remain unfortunate but unforeseeable coincidences, no matter how learned we become.

It is difficult for a young child to accept the arbitrary and there is probably little point in trying to impose the acceptance on him. When he is old enough to ask the question with some sophistication (I've talked this through with eleven-year-olds), it is from this point of view that we will have to begin.

This principle—the existence of coincidence and residual chaos in the world—and the idea discussed earlier, that Man has the moral freedom to choose between good and evil deeds and to act on his choice, are the twin pillars of our new understanding of God's relationship to the evil and suffering that exist in the world. There *are* things which the divine force we label God cannot do. He cannot act in violation of a law of Nature since one of the manifestations of God in the world resides in the orderliness and immutability of the laws of Nature. He cannot compel men to be good rather than bad, nor can He protect them from the consequences of their actions, or the consequences other people's actions have for them.

Strictly speaking, God never punishes men, if we take "punishment" to mean an unpleasant experience not stemming directly from what a person does, but inflicted from without to teach a person to refrain from the act. In the world of God and man, there is no punishment; there are only consequences. If a child plays with matches and one ignites and burns his hand—that is a consequence. If he plays with matches and his mother takes them away and slaps his hand—that is a punishment. *Punishment always involves another party's disapproval and deliberate intervention; consequences flow impersonally from the nature of an act itself.*

This means that a person who falls from the roof of a

building will probably die, no matter what his reasons were for being on the roof or falling from it. If, in one miraculous case out of a thousand, he comes out of it with nothing more than a broken leg, it is not because "God decided" that he should live while 999 others died, but is due solely to physical-natural causes.

It means that a man who exposes himself to contagious diseases runs a risk of contracting the disease, even if he is doing it for the noblest of reasons. Contagion does not distinguish between a doctor trying to stem an epidemic and a criminal burglarizing the home of a sick man.

On any number of occasions, I've gone to the hospital to visit a congregant who had been in a serious automobile accident but emerged from it with only minor injuries. Usually, the person will say something like, "If I could go through that and come out alive, there must be a God!" At the time, I'm usually not inclined to argue theology with the person, but I obviously can't accept the notion that one man survived because God chose to spare him any more that I can accept the idea that another died because God wanted him to die. Had this patient been killed in the crash, as many perfectly fine and loveable people are, would that therefore mean there is no God? Either God is real or He isn't. Either our world is built around certain possibilities and relationships, or it isn't. Only a childish notion of God-as-heavenly-Puppeteer who determines what happens to us gives us leave to "believe in God" only when a tragedy happens to someone else and to decide "there is no God" when it touches us.

God does not punish. What we gratuitously call "acts of God" are sometimes acts of destructive men and sometimes acts of blind, inflexible Nature. The obvious, and very important, question which must be asked at this point is, "If God doesn't cause these things, and if He can't prevent them, what good is He?"

What good is God in a world where tragic and undeserved fates befall people at random? Well, first of all, He gives us a stable and orderly world, a world in which things conform to regular laws, so that we can learn to understand these laws and use them. Sometimes—when a President Kennedy is shot or a relative of ours suffers from an incurable disease—we may find ourselves wishing that the natural laws of the world were less regular, that they would change in selected, worthy cases. But would we really find the world more liveable if the law of gravity sometimes applied and sometimes didn't, if the heart sometimes needed to pump blood and didn't at others, if neither physician nor scientist could get standard results from standardized procedures? Not only is there no power capable of overriding the laws of nature, but a world not based on cause and effect would be even harder to live in than a world of occasional tragedy.

Secondly, God has helped men discover ways of minimizing tragedy, through understanding and controlling Nature's laws, through learning from experience—their own and the teachings of others—which actions lead to undesirable consequences. To the extent that Man uses his intelligence and develops his conscience, he turns to

God in order to reduce chaos and misfortune. When man becomes more godly, when he spends more of his resources on medical research and care for the needy, when he no longer teaches other men to despise their neighbors and themselves, there will be fewer tragic "acts of God" on earth.

And thirdly—what good is God in a world where misfortune occurs so frequently? He gives men the power to overcome tragedy and find reasons for going on with life. He moves men to comfort the bereaved, to give each other new strength and faith. Disaster, accident, sudden death are not "acts of God." *The resolve of men to rebuild their lives after disaster is the true act of God.*

Suffering and Evil from the Child's Point of View

Misfortune and death have special meanings for the growing child, meanings we must appreciate before we can respond to his open questions and even to the questions he is afraid to ask.

Young children find the world so big and bewildering and even intimidating that they need to believe there is a power controlling it. (They not only *tend* to believe this; I suspect they *need* to.) If there is no one to control the world better than they can, they feel terribly threatened. At first, they believe their parents are all-powerful. Mother will protect them from all harm and solve all problems. Father will magically mend all broken toys, answer all questions and shield them from all danger. When they learn that their parents can do these things imperfectly, they eagerly fasten on God as being the

Superparent capable of all things.

At this stage, a child probably needs to believe in God thusly in order to feel secure about the world. His mind can't handle the idea that some things in the world are random, not subject to anyone's control; there is little use in trying to force the idea on him. In point of fact, one of the things for which the term "God" stands is the complex orderliness and fundamental goodness of the world. The youngster who starts with *that* will be able to modify it and build on it later. Problems will arise only if he never outgrows the first phase and never becomes mature enough to live with chaos and accident.

There is a very serious problem implicit in the early view of a God-parent, who is all-capable of preventing harm. Children *are* vulnerable to illness and injury and they inevitably ask themselves why God let it happen to them. Most injuries occurring to most children are minor, so that they don't take them too seriously. "You bumped your head because you weren't looking where you were going, and I hope you've learned to be more careful. God didn't do it."

But what do you say to the child who loses a parent, or is born handicapped, or is seriously crippled in an accident? How do you answer *him* when he asks, "Why did God let it happen to me?"

We must realize, first of all, that the average child views his misfortune as punishment. God has found him wanting and punishes him for something he did wrong. So strong is the compulsion to make sense of the world that a child (and a great many adults in similar situations) will invent the most far-fetched reasons to "justify" what has happened to him. Children with failing vision or physical disfigurements convince themselves that an all-knowing and impeccably-just God is punishing them for touching or looking at things they weren't supposed to, or for excessive vanity and concern with their appearance. And if the triviality of their "sin" seems to fall light-years short of the magnitude of their "punishment," they assume that "God must have His own reasons" for taking it so seriously. They might very well think so even without the elaborate machinery of traditional religion and theology—out of an inborn tendency toward "cosmic neatness." (Think of all the fairy tales in which everybody gets what he deserves at the end and of the degree to which children are troubled if "crime" and "punishment" don't work out. I suspect that they feel uneasy when they have done something wrong and haven't been caught not because they are afraid of being discovered and punished, but because sin without punishment upsets their sense of harmony in the world!) Our first responsibility, greater even than the need for logical or theological consistency, *is to maintain the child's sense of his own worth. Under no circumstances whatsoever should his religion ever be permitted to condemn him as one who has been judged and found wanting,* with his misfortune *prima facie* evidence of his unworthiness. This is the *very reverse* of the function religion should perform in a child's (or any person's) life.

"Why did God let it happen?" God doesn't *make* things happen, or *let* them happen. God does *not* judge or punish. He doesn't distribute a minimum quota of tumors and heart attacks each day, choosing His victims until He has used up a day's supply of misfortune! He doesn't mark certain people for illness and disaster, and others for health and prosperity. Things happen for natural reasons, some of which we understand and some of which we don't. The human body is a very complicated entity; many things have to go right for it to be healthy and it is easy for some little thing to go wrong. That doesn't mean God judges you and gives you "what you deserve."

"God doesn't punish people; He helps people when they get hurt. A lot of very wonderful people have bad things happen to them, sometimes through no fault of their own, sometimes because they are careless for just a little while and the laws of Nature don't make any exception because they were good people. When misfortune happens, they call upon God and find the strength and the courage to go on living and working and make the most of their situation."

"Can God put back a severed leg, or reverse the course of an incurable disease?" No, He can't. There are laws of Nature which are the same always for all people. Sometimes, an apparently incurable disease does suddenly disappear, but it happens so rarely and arbitrarily—and not necessarily to the most religious or most moral people or to those who could contribute most to the world—that we can't say, "God has chosen to intervene."

God does give men the intelligence and the desire to help others—so that they invent artificial limbs and search for drugs to cure or slow down disease. He gives the suffering person and his family the strength to console each other and go on living.

How do you answer a child who sees a blind man or a cripple in the street, and asks, "What happened to him?"

I am told that there is a folk proverb among Middle Eastern peasants: "If you see a blind man, kick him; why should you be kinder than God?" And I have often contrasted this with the outlook of the Torah: *"You shall not set a stumbling block before the blind."* The difference is not only one of good manners but one of theological assumptions. If you believe that God causes everything in this world and if you also believe Him to be a just and moral God, then you must follow these assumptions to their logical conclusion: that people get what they deserve and that therefore misfortune is divine punishment. (Unless you prefer the grotesque absurdity that God afflicts some people with blindness so as to provide others with opportunities for charity.) This puts charity and compassion on very uncertain footing: why, indeed, should we be "kinder than God?" Helping those whom God has chosen to afflict would be uncalled for, perhaps even rebelling against His will. Once we free ourselves of the obligation to explain every calamity as God's will, as justified in His sight, we are free to say that misfortunes befall men for all sorts of reasons—some of human origin, some accidental. The most useful question for our purposes is not, "Why did it happen?" but, "Now that it has happened, what can we do about it?"

To a child whose curiosity is aroused by the cripple or the blind man we can only say, "I don't know what happened. Maybe he was born that way, or maybe he had an accident. If you think he was punished for doing something wrong, I don't. He may be a very fine person to whom this happened for reasons we don't understand. Most people, you know, don't have that happen to them. They have their eyes, their arms and legs all their lives. A few people do have these problems, but I think it's wonderful that they manage to lead a full and active life and only occasionally need help from us."

The point about such tragedies not happening to most people is more important than it might appear at first glance. When children ask about the physically handicapped, I don't think they are drawn to ask solely because of instinctive compassion. I think, rather, they have become aware of their own vulnerability and are alarmed by it. (That's why it is often difficult to make children act compassionately toward the disfigured or the very old and senile. They are frightened of them and of the danger they represent—that something similar may happen to them. Young children are very much concerned about the vulnerability of their own bodies—insisting, for example, on band-aids to hide and conceal broken skin. This is a natural, probably even a healthy, response for children, but may lead to difficulties in teaching them to react to the afflicted without panic.)

We can't guarantee that accidents won't happen to them, and we want them to take seriously the need to use tools and cross streets carefully, but we can reassure them by pointing out that such tragedies happen to very few people. We can protect the dignity of the victims of misfortune by emphasizing that it is definitely not a divine punishment visited on people who have done wrong.

To summarize: God does not cause everything that happens in the world. Some things are the result of sheer accident, others are caused by men exercising their freedom in a harmful way.

God does not punish. Some people suffer as a direct result of their actions, but natural laws operate without making moral judgments. What God does is to provide resources of strength and faith for the victims of misfortune and resources of compassion for those around them, so that together they can go on living and building a life in spite of what happened.

Children and Death

If children respond to a chance encounter with a cripple by becoming anxious about their own physical vulnerability, their awareness of death alarms them even more. Once again, we adults are often of little help to them when they really need us because so often we ourselves haven't thought through our own feelings about death.

If there is one fact we should learn from the collective experience of the human race, it is that death is inevitable. Every human being is mortal: he will die, probably not at a time and in a place of his own choosing—and probably sooner than those close to him would have wished. While we know this to be true abstractly, we don't really learn to live with the knowledge.

We remain terribly squeamish about the fact of death.

When we keep children away from funerals and send them to stay with neighbors during the first days of mourning, we tell ourselves that we are "protecting" them from some of the unpleasant realities they needn't confront as yet. (I know of a 15-year-old girl who was considered "too young" to attend her grandfather's funeral.) In truth, I think that *we* are probably "protecting" *ourselves* from having to teach them about death and mortality, because we don't know what to say. Apparently, telling youngsters about "the facts of death" leads to as much vagueness and inarticulate stammering as telling them about "the facts of life."

When we avoid telling our children about death, we are actually telling them something very undesirable—namely, that death is too terrible for even a mature adult to face. When we get them out of the house during the week of mourning, when we become flustered at their questions, when we overreact emotionally to the whole subject . . . we make our children just as incapable of confronting this inevitable fact of living as we are.

What do children really want to know about death? I can't believe they are concerned with the subtle concept of their own non-existence. The death of an adult on the periphery of a child's world—a grandparent, an aunt or uncle, a friend's parent—does not really raise abstract questions of divine justice and human mortality. Instead, it presents the very real threat to *his own* immediate world, the danger that *his own* parents may die and leave him without their very necessary and comforting presence. The child who is prompted by peripheral death to ask his mother, "Why do people die?" is really asking,

"Are *you* going to die and leave me alone?" Even if he doesn't actually betray this concern in his question, we might do well to anticipate it in our answer.

(A 12-year-old boy I know, after the death of his grandfather, became very upset when he saw his parents smoking, when he heard them complain of not feeling well, or when they were out late and didn't return on time. He would go into his parents' bedroom in the middle of the night, saying he couldn't sleep because he was thinking of grandpa. In reality, he was checking to make sure they were still there.)

We might say something like this: "People die for many reasons. Sometimes people get very old and tired. They've done everything they had to do in life. And after they've lived a long, long time, dying puts an end to the story of their life." (Note: don't put too much emphasis on people being tired or sick as a prelude to their death, lest the child be terrified, whenever he is ill or tired, by the thought that he may be dying.) We can speak of a grandparent's life as a beautiful story. "Sometimes when you're listening to a good story, you wish it would go on forever. But you know the story has to end. The story of grandma's life is over, and all we can do is remember it and be grateful that we were part of it."

"If you are worried about Daddy or Mommy dying, please don't. It's very unusual. Most children have their parents around until well after they are able to be on their own, until they grow up and get married and have their own children and don't need their parents as much any more. And besides, Daddy and Mommy will try to take good care of ourselves and of our health."

In the event a parent should die, leaving young children, our task of comforting and consoling them is immense. It probably can't be done as well as we would like to do it. But we might start by playing down the question of, "Why did it happen?" and emphasizing instead, "What are we going to do about it now?" Let us say to the child: "This is a terrible, painful thing that has happened to you. There is nothing we can do to bring your father back. Short of that, we will try to help you and make you feel better in every way we can. You still have a lot of friends who care about you and want to see you grow up strong and happy."

By all means, let us avoid any suggestion whatsoever that God is judging either the parent or the child, or that this having happened is in any way right or good. Let us avoid cliches like, "God has His reasons" or "Maybe it's better this way." A bereaved family may have the right to find comfort in telling itself that "at least, he didn't suffer, or is no longer suffering." But strangers have no right to fall back on that.

Let us stress, rather, that the deceased was a fine person, that his death is, in fact, a tragedy, not an example of God's righteous wrath. Let us assure the bereaved child that *he* is still a good and loved person. Many people shun the victim of a tragedy as if bereavement were contagious. (I imagine they do it out of embarrassment, out of not knowing what to say.) But this only strengthens the guilt-fantasies of the child (or husband or wife or parent): "I'm responsible for this death because I was a bad person and had hateful thoughts. God found me out and punished me and now everybody knows what I am and they're punishing and avoiding me too."

And by all means, let us avoid that preposterous cliche, "The good die young." Aside from its being untrue, I can think of few things better calculated to make being good unattractive and frightening to a sensitive young child. Among its, for the most part, amusing contents, the slim volume *More Children's Letters to God* contains this touching missive:

"Dear God, Do good people have to die young? I heard my mommy say that. I'm not always good. Yours truly, Barbara."

The death of a child brings home to a youngster the very difficult and severely disquieting news of his own vulnerability, the fact that little children may indeed die. He may see the playmate's death as a punishment and fear that he will be the next to suffer for having done similar things. Here too, we might give a similar answer: "Yes, sometimes people do die when they're children, but it's very unusual, and it's *always* an accidental thing, *never* a punishment for being bad. But it's very rare; most children live to become grown-ups. They get sick, but they get well again. They hurt themselves, but they heal. And they go on to have a long and full life."

"What Does It Feel Like to Die?"

(Need it be said that we should not put this question into a child's mind. There is no need to deal with it unless the child specifically asks it or plays the situation out in his fantasies and manifests concern.)

I suspect the child is afraid death is painful. He is unable to move or speak, but he is conscious of what people are doing to him and saying about him. People will close him up in a box and bury him and he will be unable to protest—a frightening enough prospect. We might tell him that being dead is different from playing dead. One doesn't see, hear or feel anything at all. The dead person is through with feeling pain or anything else. He doesn't know that he is being buried. We bury people so that there will be a particular place to which we can go to think about them.

"Where Do People Go When They Die?"

The first and most honest answer to this question is that we don't know; nobody knows. No one who ever died has been able to tell those left behind what happened to him.

In fact, telling the living what happened in death would be impossible, because when people die they no longer see or feel or know anything. They don't feel uncomfortable about being put in a coffin or buried. They can't hear what we say about them. What *does* happen to them? The body of a dead person is put into the ground very respectfully, in a special place called a cemetery.

When he was alive, the person was more than a body. He was also what we call a soul, a personality. He was good at certain things; he cared about certain things and certain people. Things happened to him and he remembered them. All this made up his soul, the part of him that wasn't his body, that let him be him and nobody else. The question of what happens to a soul is a very hard one to answer, because a soul isn't a thing, a physical object which has to be in one place or another. A soul is a little bit like God—not an object, but a way of thinking and feeling, of making certain things happen. Asking, "Where does the soul go when a man dies?" is a little like asking "Where does the light go when you turn the switch off?" A soul doesn't *go* anywhere; it just isn't there any more, because the things which made it possible have been taken away.

And yet, if a man was a good person and people loved him, even after his body has died and been buried, people will still remember him. They will talk about him and be slightly different people because of what he meant to them. And if they remember him and act differently because of it, maybe that is the answer to where his soul went.

When people we care about are alive, but physically distant from us, when a child's parents are at work or away on a trip, we can think of them and feel their presence and it is a little bit as if they were with us. This is what the power of love and memory can do. Let us be comforted by the thought that, even when people are dead, we can summon up memories of them and feel them close.

Early in the history of religion, people found it hard to believe that when a person died that was the end of his life and they would never see him again. It wasn't enough for them to remember him and tell others about him. So they made up stories about a place where souls went after death. In this place, the souls looked the way the people had looked on earth. And when the other members of their family died years later, their souls would go to this place—heaven—and recognize each other and be reunited there.

Of course, they had no way of knowing that there really was such a place, any more than we have of knowing that there isn't. None of us can say for sure. A lot of very fine people, Jews and non-Jews, have believed in a heaven and many still do today. But there are reasons for being skeptical. Firstly, people invented the story because they *wanted* to believe they would see their relatives again, not because they had any real reasons to think they would. Secondly, if the soul isn't a thing, if it is a non-physical object, how can one really talk about a "place where non-physical objects go and recognize and talk to each other?" A soul detached from a body can't see or hear, nor can it feel happy or sad, because these emotions depend on physical reactions. Besides, people who believe that souls go to heaven usually picture them looking the way people did on earth, so that they recognize each other and this raises problems. If on earth, a person was very fat or had only one arm, would he always be a fat or one-armed soul in heaven? If a man died young, leaving children who lived to normal life spans, how would they all eventually appear in heaven? A young father-soul? An old son-soul? A grandchild-soul older than his grandfather? It's understandable that people should want what was most precious in their relatives to live on, but the most reasonable assumption is that their souls continue to live on here on earth only in the memories and actions of other people. Fundamentally, Judaism at its most profound has always taught us to take *this* world seriously, to try and live a full and rich and satisfying life in this world and let speculation about where the soul goes afterwards, if it goes anywhere at all, remain speculation.

Reward and Punishment

Long ago, people speculated on souls living on after death, not only because they wanted to see their loved ones again, but for another very important reason. Life on earth seemed so unfair. Some people lived good and righteous lives, but suffered one misfortune after another —illness, bereavement, business reverses. Others seemed to "get away with murder." It was tempting to believe the story did not end with death, to think that beyond the grave there was another world where the good were given rewards more glorious than the ones they missed in this life and where the wicked were at last punished (or at least denied reward.)

Again, we have no way of actually knowing whether such a world exists. We can only be skeptical, try to find our answers in terms of this life and not depend on anything beyond it.

Are the good rewarded and the bad punished in this world? God does not punish, nor does He reward. He does not intervene in this world to pin medals on people or to change the consequences of their deeds to fit their moral deserts. However, He has given us a world in which certain things *lead* to good consequences while others *lead* to bad ones. If a dishonest businessman loses the confidence of his customers or is exposed, shamed and sent to prison, it isn't because God is punishing him. It's simply the result of his own wrong behavior. If that same businessman is never caught, it's not because God is "neglecting to punish him" as he deserves.

It is, however, all too obvious that, if we measure reward and punishment in terms of health, wealth, comfort and length of days, the most deserving people aren't always rewarded, nor are the immoral ones always punished. We should certainly acknowledge this fact. This is the way the world really is and we serve no good purpose in trying to explain it away, either by denying that the people are good or by denying that bankruptcy and illness are misfortunes.

Why does God let these injustices happen? Well, God isn't in the business of letting them happen or preventing them. Some happen because men are less just and less kind than they might be; others happen for reasons we can't begin to comprehend: I cannot believe that "God's will" is one of them.

But there are other currencies in which people may be rewarded or punished: growth of character, satisfaction, clear conscience, the esteem of friends, a good name to bequeath to children, the expectation that their children will grow up with moral values and above all, a sense of having realized one's potential as that rarest of creatures, an authentic human being. Many people who lack affluence, comfort and perfect health have these other satisfactions and find them reward enough.

It would be nice if this were a world where good people were protected from misfortune and bad people marked for some punishment beyond their troubled consciences and the enmity of their neighbors, punishment from which they may or may not suffer. Virtue would be much more attractive in such a world and vice much less tempting. Unfortunately this isn't the world we live in, and we must face that fact. God isn't a master Marionettist, pulling strings and making everything happen—only by the most extreme moral and intellectual contortions can we contend that He is. In this world, the finest human beings are prone to illness and accident and to moments of selfishness and stupidity as well. The life of any one of us is hazardous and difficult and sooner or later will end. What can God do for us within these limitations? He can't change the "ground rules," either for individuals or for the human race as a whole. But He can help us to know what those ground rules are and can lead us to discover where real satisfaction can be found, how to measure success accurately. He can help us find the faith and the strength to go on living in this world, no matter how unfairly it may treat us, because it is still the only one we have and still capable of yielding satisfaction.

"Why Does God Make Bad People?"

God doesn't make people bad. God creates people—that is, He makes it possible for people to be born with certain abilities and options—and then leaves the question of what sort of people they want to be up to them.

Some people use the choice and the power they have for good, and some use it for evil.

Actually, to be truly accurate, we must point out that there are no "good people" and "bad people," that everybody does a *mixture* of good and bad things in his life, that "good people" occasionally do things which hurt or disappoint others and that "bad people" aren't bad *all* the time.

Even when we remove the responsibility for making "bad people" from God, we still haven't answered the child's question. He doesn't really want to know about God; he wants to know why there *are* bad people, that is, why some people choose to do bad things. This is a very serious question for him.

We must admit, at the outset, that we don't really know what makes people tick. Why some people choose to be good and others decide to do evil things is one of the great puzzles of human life. However, people who have spent a lot of time studying the question and thinking about it have some suggestions.

Sometimes people do bad things because they are angry. They feel bad about something that has happened to them, so they don't care if they get into more trouble or if they make somebody else feel bad.

Sometimes people do things they shouldn't do because they just don't know any better, because no one ever told them that such things are wrong, or because they don't realize what will happen to them or to somebody else if they do them. We don't consider such people bad, but we do expect them to learn from their mistakes and to know better the next time.

Sometimes people do bad things because they are not sure that they are as strong or as clever or as brave as they would like to be. So they hurt someone or they trick someone and think it makes them feel stronger or more clever. It usually doesn't help them for very long. A bully is most often a child who is afraid that he isn't as strong or as brave as he would like to be, so he has to keep trying to prove how strong he is by picking on others. Then he wonders why the other children don't like him.

Sometimes people do bad things because, somewhere along the way, someone told them that they were "no good" and they believed it. They don't think they are capable of doing good things and so they don't try. Maybe they once tried to do something good and it didn't work and they were made to feel so bad about failing that they are just afraid to try being good anymore.

Just about everybody feels like doing something bad at one time or another, but most people don't pay attention to the feeling. They are strong enough and they believe in their own ability to be good, so they don't do evil things, no matter how tempting they are. The really strong child is never a bully and the really brave one is never a show-off, because they don't always have to prove how strong and brave they are.

What happens to bad people? Some of them, if they do very bad things, are caught and punished. Most of them feel bad and disappointed in themselves, whether they get caught or not. And all of them miss out on the greatest satisfaction that there is in life—the satisfaction of knowing you are living the way people are meant to live.

We might ask at this point: Is it fair to give God credit for the good things people do and not hold Him responsible for the bad? Is it intellectually honest to see Him as the Power that makes love, justice and generosity possible, but not as the Power that makes hatred and cruelty possible? Or is this an example of what one theologian calls "religious gerrymandering," in which we define God so as to include only the qualities we want?

Let us remember that God is not an entity out in space somewhere, whose nature we have to explore and describe accurately. "God" is a name we give to a certain set of realities that we have discovered to be built into the world. We do not start with a definition of God and deduce conclusions about the world from it. We start with life and our responses to life and let those responses lead us to an understanding of God.

In Hebrew we read from right to left, and perhaps in theology we ought to read from right to left also. When we see a statement like "God is good, God is forgiving," let us not take it as a description of a person named God who lives in Heaven. Read it backwards: goodness is godly, forgiveness is godly. These and all the other qualities we associate with God are manifestations of the godly in our lives.

In a sense, God does "make hatred possible," even as He makes love possible, because He does not make love and kindness inevitable. Man is born free to choose his path. We say that when man exerts himself to be honest, loving, and truthful, he calls upon the Power we know as

God to help him grow. When man chooses to be mean and selfish, he does not call on any demonic Power of Evil, nor does he call on "God's bad aspects." He simply lives without God and so lives a restricted and far less satisfying life.

The child who sees that evil goes unpunished is troubled by something else as well—by the implied threat to his own conscience and his own will power. It would be much easier to be good, to resist temptation, if he could be sure that God was "watching," just as the child finds it easier to do his homework if he knows that the teacher checks it carefully and grades it fairly. He would be less apt to resent the evildoer, who gives in to temptation when he struggles and manages to resist, if he could be sure that the miscreant would "get what's coming to him." If restraint brings no reward and transgression no punishment, the child finds it that much harder to restrain himself and asks, "What's the point of knocking myself out to be good?"

Our answer to this very serious question will vary with the age and maturity of the child, but in essence all of our answers will be variations on the same point. God's justice may be a blunt instrument rather than a precise scalpel, but essentially there is a divine justice, however imprecise, in the world. No good deed is ever wasted; it always leaves you a better person. No transgression is ever really escaped from; its punishment, in one form or another, always follows. A thief or fraudulent businessman may not be caught and sent to prison (though many, even most, of them are), but he may be "punished" in other ways. (The quotation marks indicate that his fate may not be punishment, strictly speaking, but will be the immediate consequences of his dishonesty.) The man who lives by dishonesty, for instance, lives in fear of being exposed and caught. He becomes suspicious of other people, even of his closest friends and associates, suspecting that they are doing to him what he would do them and what he knows they have done to others. It seems to me that having to go through life, the only life we will ever have, without ever being able to relax and trust the people around us, without ever knowing the satisfactions of self-control, generosity and self-esteem, is all the punishment we would wish anyone.

Isaac Bashevis Singer has written a short story called, "The Brooch" about a skillful professional thief who rationalizes his thievery to himself and tells himself that he is really as good as anyone else, until the day comes when his whole world falls apart. He discovers that his wife has learned the art of thievery from him and finds he can no longer trust or respect her. He learns that his daughters are social outcasts at school, suspected of robbery anytime anything is lost or missing. This man, who was so sure he had gotten away with all his thefts, suddenly finds his punishment more than he can take and leaves his home to work in a tannery, returning to the arduous but honest living he could never take seriously before.

There can be only one answer to a child's question, "Does it make a difference if I'm a good person?" It very definitely does. It may not make a difference in how long you live, how rich or famous you become, but it makes a big difference—*all the difference*—in what you think of yourself, what others think of you, how satisfying you find life and what sort of memories you leave behind when your life is over.

But doesn't the prayerbook, in the *Rosh HaShanah* service say that *"all creatures pass in review before the Almighty,"* and that, *"on this day it is decided who shall live and who shall die, who shall be wealthy and who shall be poor?"*

Yes, it does. Because at the time the prayer was composed, people took the metaphor of God as judge and the idea of divine justice so literally that they pictured God as meting out every individual's fate in the same way that a human judge decides what a person's sentence will be. They managed to ignore or evade or rationalize the manifest injustices which occurred between one *Rosh HaShanah* and the next.

We can no longer accept this hyper-literal conception of God as the dispenser of Justice, nor can we accept their understanding of a system of reward and punishment which so conspicuously fails to fit the facts. Nor can we accept an idea of predestination which tells us that what we will choose to do next April or May has already been "decided" by a force outside ourselves last September. But we can take this ancient prayer as an annual reminder that justice—meting out to every man what he deserves—is an aspect of divinity, that when we make this world more just we are being God-like and that the decisions and commitments we make for ourselves on those days devoted especially to self-examination may well determine the future course of our lives. They won't decide whether we will live through twelve more months, whether our health will be good, or whether our businesses will prosper. But they may determine what our lives—however long—will *mean* and in what terms we will measure the success and wealth which we and others may attain.

Prayers for Healing

Late one evening, my phone rang. "Rabbi, my mother is going in for an operation tomorrow. Would you say a prayer for her?" Can I really believe that the words I recite will have an influence on the recovery of a woman I have never met, a woman who doesn't know of my existence, let alone my prayers on her behalf? More than that, can I believe in a God who has the power to cure a sick person but who will exercise that power only if we recite the right words at the right time in the right language, a God who will let a person die if, in our confusion, we forget the prayer or get the words wrong?

The problem of prayer in relation to God as we have come to understand Him is a difficult one and will be dealt with at length later. But prayers for healing are in a separate category, and will be discussed here, in the context of considering a God who does not reward or punish or intervene to set aside the workings of Nature.

"Oh God, please cure her!" is not really a request, much as it sounds like one. It is a cry of pain, an expression of helplessness, of the finiteness of human wisdom in the face of illness and death. God "answers" such a cry not by sending a miraculous recovery, but by giving the one who cries out enough strength to bear his burden, however heavy it may become. I usually respond to requests like the one made of me that evening by saying, "I'll pray for your mother's recovery, so that you and she will know that the community is with you and hopes things turn out well for you. And I hope that you will pray too. Not just for a recovery. Pray that you'll be strong enough and your mother and all your family will be strong enough to take whatever comes, without being broken by it. Pray that, if things turn out well, you'll remember to be grateful and appreciate life and health more. Pray that you find comfort in the knowledge that skilled, dedicated doctors and nurses—strangers to you—are working to make her better, because God has given them minds to understand and hearts to care about the pain of a fellow human being. If you can find comfort in the fact that you have done everything you could do and the doctors are doing everything they can, if you are strong enough to accept the worst and be humbly grateful for anything better, then your prayers will have been answered."

In the time of the *Mishnah* (compiled around the year 200 C.E.), it was already forbidden for a man who saw smoke coming from a burning building to pray, "God, let it not be my house!" Not only is it a distortion of religion to implore God to cause someone else's house to burn rather than yours, but such a prayer is a defiance of logic and reality. A certain house was *already* aflame, and it was *already* too late for God, or any other power, to decide which house it was.

Similarly—from the standpoint of strict logic—when one is waiting for the results of a medical examination, it makes no sense to pray, "Let it turn out to be something not too serious." The condition either already exists or does not exist and will not disappear through the intervention of our words. If things could be changed thusly, no one would ever fall seriously ill, for every person would recite such a prayer with the utmost sincerity.

Yet we do utter such prayers at such times, almost instinctively, and as long as we don't seriously expect them to alter the course of a patient's health, they may be desirable as an outlet for our strong emotions and concerns.

What prayer can we offer when we or someone close to us is ill? First, our prayers can affirm the essential goodness and helpfulness of the world. For this is not a fatalistic world where certain courses are decreed beforehand and tragedy is the foreordained fate of certain men. Things may work out well; they very often do. The sun shines more often than not. Most people recover from most illnesses; most operations are successful; most children survive the dangers of their vulnerable years, grow to adulthood, marry and have children of their own. In many cases, the percentages will be heavily on our side; in almost all others, at least the possibility of a happy ending will be there.

Secondly, in our prayers, we should be grateful for the

God-given skills and dedication of those who try to help us in our illness. God has given men minds sharp enough to unravel the mysteries of illness and track down their cures. He has given them souls so great that doctors and nurses, who were virtual strangers to us until now, are willing to sacrifice their comfort, perhaps even risk their own health—in a way for which no fee can really compensate—in order to help us. Our prayers would express gratitude not only for the existence of medical science, but for its embodiment in these particular men and women.

Beyond this, there is the consideration that our prayers for another's health and recovery will come to that person's attention and strengthen his spirits with the knowledge that others are concerned about him.

And lastly, no prayer in time of illness would be complete without articulating the hope that, should things go badly, should we come out of the ordeal crippled or bereaved, we will find within ourselves the strength to live with that result too. We all know examples of people whose experience of pain and illness, their own or a relative's, has left them badly hurt. But they were able, nevertheless, to call upon God for the strength to go on living in His world and believing in it. We might pray that, should we find ourselves in such a position, we will be capable of showing the same strength and faith.

This, of course, is the message of the Mourner's *Kaddish*, which Judaism bids the bereaved recite. We have no "prayers for the dead" in Judaism—we have prayers for the living, in which those who have been hurt by life proclaim publicly that they can still believe in God and in His world.

We can deal with the prayers of children, prayers growing out of their frustration at not being able to do more for the sake of someone they care about, on the basis of this understanding. "Don't expect things to work out just because you prayed sincerely. Pray for the strength to take what comes and to appreciate the efforts being made. And whatever happens, you can be sure that grandma, or whoever you were praying for, was made happier at a difficult time of her life, by the knowledge that you cared about her so much."

On the very day I wrote these lines, a member of my congregation called me to tell me of the death of her son, who had been institutionalized with irreparable brain damage since birth. She told me, in the course of the conversation, what her young daughter had said when she heard of her brother's death: "I guess all those coins we dropped in the wishing well didn't help."

An answer to such a child at such a time might be something like this: "I think we knew all along that they wouldn't help, if by helping, you mean that a miracle might happen and Larry would suddenly be all well. But they helped in other ways. They were our way of saying something that was in our hearts—that we cared about Larry and felt so bad there wasn't more we could do to help him lead a normal life, that we hadn't given up hope some doctor might yet discover a new cure. And last of all, remember where all those coins went—to help other sick children for whom there was more that could be done. Because we cared about Larry and because we knew how the family of a very sick child feels, we were moved to do something to help them."

Chapter V

GOD AND THE BIBLE

MOST OF THE QUESTIONS with which we have dealt until
now have stemmed from life situations. They have issued
from the hopes, fears and experiences of children growing up. These children were moved to ask about them
and we tried to answer.

There is another category of questioning, however,
which would never have arisen in a child's mind unless
we had first set the stage for it—questions based, not on
life experiences but on Bible stories, history lessons, holi-
day observances. And we must be prepared to deal with
these too.

Our children encounter Bible stories at Hebrew school.
They will read them in children's books and see them on
television. These stories introduce them to a world where
God speaks to man and arranges to give him what he
deserves. They enter a world where extraordinary things
are constantly happening. As we have suggested, these
stories are too profound and too conspicuously a part of
the child's Jewish heritage for us to omit, rewrite or censor,
but there are two dangers for which we must be on the
alert. The first is that child may reject the stories out of
hand because of their mythological components and lose
all respect for religion as a whole along with them. Or he
may accept them literally and unquestioningly, ultimately

resenting and feeling threatened by any interpretation of religion which clashes with the world of the Bible tales which he remembers.

The former is the greater danger in the case of bright, perceptive children, children for whom education is an active, liberating encounter rather than a matter of passive acceptance. These are the children to whom all disciplines of life, including religion, will one day turn for creative leadership and it would be tragic for them to reject religion scornfully as a collection of fairy tales to be taken seriously only by the simple-minded. These bright children are quick to spot contradictions and inconsistencies and to measure claims against experience. They are less likely to let two contradictory ideas co-exist in their minds solely because this is what they understood the teacher to be saying. Bright children will be perplexed by the "unscientific," sometimes misleading picture of the universe as it emerges from the pages of the Bible. They will be disturbed to the point of outrage at the "immoral" behavior of some of its heroes, which we will hard-pressed to justify. And they will be unable or unwilling to listen attentively to the rest of the Biblical message because of the framework in which it is presented, unless we come up with satisfying answers to their challenges.

Parents and teachers have to learn that it is not enough for our children to "know the Bible," to be familiar with its contents and with the names and deeds of its heroes. More thorough acquaintance with it may only give them additional reasons to think of it as antiquated and irrelevant. If our children are to accept the Bible as the cornerstone of Israel's existence as a people and as the fundamental document of their own faith, we have to teach them *how* to study the Bible (the Jew *studies* the Bible; he doesn't just read it to see how the story turns out), *why* they should study it and what information they can legitimately seek to learn from it pages.

Genesis vs. Geology

Somewhere around the level of the fifth grade, the typical Jewish youngster, who has dutifully put in his time attending religious school, undergoes a traumatic experience. He is given an account of how the world came into being, an account which conflicts with the beautiful, poetic account of Creation he has read in the Bible. This new account is given authoritatively and buttressed by scientific evidence bearing on the age of rocks and fossils and the immense lapses of time that separated one stage of development from another. Moreover, the world and the living things in it are pictured as having evolved naturally, blindly and automatically, not as having been fashioned by God.

How does the child resolve the conflict? His public school teacher is firm in telling him that the Biblical story is what people believed before Science discovered the truth. His religious leaders are less likely to tell him with equal fervor that the scientific view is false and the Biblical account the accurate one. There may still be a few such teachers around: I once heard one tell a class that, just as God created Man middle-aged and not an infant, so did He create "middle-aged" rocks and fossils, whose carbon-14 datings went back to a period before the earth existed. And why did He do this? To test people of a later age, to see whether they would accept the word of God over that of some laboratory technician!

It is more likely that the defender of the Biblical story will react with stammering embarrassment and vagueness and explain that the scientific explanation is right, but the Bible teaches the same thing in other words. "Who says a day was 24 hours long in those times? Who knows how long one of God's working days is? Doesn't the Psalmist say, '*A thousand years in Your sight are but as a day that is past.*' Maybe the day to which Genesis refers was five million years long?"

Let us consider the effects of such an answer. To a person who wants to continue believing in the Bible and asks only that such belief be made intellectually respectable, this kind of harmonization may help. But a person without such commitment is likely to find it no reason for taking the Bible seriously. If the Bible tells us exactly what Science does, but more confusingly and with less detail, why not get our information directly from Science and avoid the risk of misunderstanding the Biblical account?

We do better to reply that the two accounts don't tell the same story in different words, but neither do they conflict. They tell us different things about the same subject—our world and how it came to be—each speaking from its own vantage point and pursuing its own purposes.

Geology tells us, objectively and without value judgments, *what* happened, how the world came into being. It describes the development of continents, the formation of mountains, rivers and plains, the successive encroachments of the glaciers on the more temperate climates. Science traces the evolution of amphibian animals from fish, the evolution of mammals and ultimately the emergence of man. It shows us how very slow and painstaking a process this was. The opening chapter of Genesis has no quarrel with any aspect of this account. Genesis teaches the modern reader not only points of fact, but value judgments about those facts; it tells us not what happened but *what it means for us*. Genesis cannot be expected to serve us as a geology, anthropology, or biology text. Anyone who tries to find anthropology or geology in it will end up learning bad anthropology and bad geology. Genesis is a religious book (not a very revolutionary idea, to be sure, but too often overlooked in the Battle of Darwin's Theory) and we read it for religious enlightenment, not physics.

Science can give us abundant evidence of the world's being complex and orderly and this is very important. But *only* a religious description of the complex and orderly world can properly call it "good," that is, hospitable to the qualities a man needs to develop if he is to become fully human.

Science tells us wherein Man is similar to other mammals and wherein he is different, that he has a prehensile thumb, a talent for conceptualizing, a highly developed language. Only religion can crystallize this difference by stating that Man is fashioned *"in the image of God,"* uniquely possessing the ability to make his life human and satisfying by developing those latent qualities which the Jewish tradition calls "divine." No scientific document can speak in these terms and remain a scientific document; yet this religious concept is at least as important for our full understanding of what a Man is as is the biological story of his emergence from among the primates.

Science can define *Homo Sapiens;* religion can envision what it means to be authentically human. The scientific mind knows that water is composed of two parts hydrogen and one part oxygen and that it is necessary for certain vital processes. The religious soul responds to the idea that water symbolizes spiritual as well as phyical cleansing and that its ritual use liberates certain feelings and energies, an idea which may be less susceptible to proof, but it no less important for full and complete living.

Science can provide us with an objective, factual account of what the world has been, which is certainly important for us to know and which should not be downgraded. Religion can give us a highly subjective, value-oriented picture of what the world is supposed to become, which is at least as important.

Who was the first man? We don't know; neither the scientist nor the rabbi can answer that question authoritatively. If he had a name, which is unlikely, it probably wasn't Adam. But it probably wasn't *Pithecanthropus Erectus* either. A scientist, in the interests of precision, is justified in coining a long Latin name, but if I were fashioning a story about what the world is all about and how man fits into it, suitable for young children and un-

sophisticated adults, I would probably do what the
Biblical narrator did and simply call the first man, *"Man"*
(which is what *Adam* means in Hebrew.)

Perhaps the editors of Genesis *thought* they were teaching anthropological data as well as religious values. They
wove into their narratives the best information at their
disposal on how the world and its inhabitants came to be.
Looking back over several thousand years of human
history, we realize how much we have learned about the
physical history of the world since their time. And perhaps,
in moments of humility, we also realize how far we still
have to go to match their sensitivity to the moral dimen-
sions of the world and their alertness to its possibilities.
This is our key to reading the Creation story and to much
of the rest of the Bible: that it is a mixture of ancient
science, since superseded, and moral insight, which
remains valid. Though it is written in the past tense, as
history, it teaches little about what the world has been,
but a great deal about what it might be.

All in all, though Genesis and geology tell different
stories about the origins of the world and the human race,
they don't conflict, nor do we have to reject one in order
to accept the other. Each is designed to answer a different
set of questions—geology being a factual description of
what happened, Genesis being a religious poem about
what the Creation of the World and the uniqueness of
Man can mean for our time. We get into difficulty only
when we try to take Genesis as a description of *what happened* (because its scientific outlook has been superseded),
or when we try to draw moral conclusions from scientific

findings and hypotheses (because that is not the purpose of scientific inquiry.)

Who Wrote the Bible? Where Did We Get It?
Did God Tell People What to Write?

The Bible, first of all, is not a book, but a collection of books. The *Torah* frequently seems to assert that it was dictated to Moses by God. The words of the classical prophets are purported to have been put in their mouths by God. While this is a simple and straightforward enough view, we cannot easily accept it. Nor can we ask our children to accept it, for several reasons.

Firstly our understanding of God does not allow Him to play the part of a Ventriloquist, speaking through the person of Isaiah or Jeremiah, nor for Him to dictate Hebrew sentences for His stenographer Moses to write down. Secondly, our studies of Biblical material indicate that even a single book of the Bible (and especially the *Torah,* the first five books) is composed of several different strata, written by different hands in different times and under different circumstances and welded into a single entity.

If we don't tell our children that the Bible is a transcription of God's word, what shall we tell them? How did the Bible come to be?

"The Bible was created by many men over a period of many, many years. We don't know the names of the men and it really doesn't matter, because they didn't make up what they wrote in the way an author today creates (or thinks he creates) his own material. They wrote down stories, ideas, memories which the people of Israel had passed on from generation to generation. The most important stories and ideas, the ones they wanted to be sure everyone remembered in the right way, became the Bible, a body of national literature which describes the world, God's place in the world and His involvement with the Jewish people."

"Did God write it? Does it contain His words?" Not in the sense that He dictated words and men wrote them down. God isn't a person with mouth, tongue and vocal cords. *People* thought of these stories and wrote them down. But in a sense, they *are* God's word. He inspired people to have ideas about how men should live. He helped people understand things that neither they nor anyone else had understood before—that certain courses are right and necessary and others wrong. And He inspired people to put these ideas into stories that are heard and never forgotten. God doesn't speak to people the way a teacher speaks to a class or a man dictates to his secretary. He inspires people to know things they never realized they knew.

"It is a little bit like when you suddenly get a wonderful idea, or suddenly come up with an answer for something, or understand something before anyone else understands it. God is the Power that lets you do these things, but when you put your idea, which He let you come up with, into words, are they your words or His words? In a way, they are both yours and His."

This, by the way, is how we can understand the term Revelation—not as God actively communicating something to us, but as our suddenly clearly seeing something we had never seen that way before, as an instance of the power we call God at work within us. Martin Buber and other thinkers have written of Revelation in this vein, as confrontation, as understanding something when you come face to face with it, even if no specific details are communicated. For example, a father looking down on his newborn child gets a message from the confrontation. He comes to understand that certain satisfactions are now open to him, certain responsibilities have just devolved on him and certain concerns are suddenly his. No one tells him any of this—least of all the infant—but he understands it in a very personal way, as he never could have understood it previously, because he brings his whole self to the confrontation.

Something similar may have happened at Mt. Sinai and at every other point in the Bible when we read, *"God spoke to Moses"* or *"the word of the Lord came to Jeremiah."* A sensitive soul, confronting the world, suddenly realized what that world needed and was inspired to put this true and valid insight into speech and writing. The result is the magnificently inspired collection of valid insights about living which we call the Bible.

We can understand the prophets in this manner too. They were not men who predicted the future, nor did they play ventriloquist's dummies for God's message. They were men of unusual spiritual sensitivity who viewed what was happening in the world around them and understood, as few of their neighbors understood, what had to be done about it.

Is the Bible True?

It depends, of course, on what we mean by "true." The stories in the Bible may be true in the sense that they say something valid and accurate about life, but not in the sense that they describe actual events as they actually happened. Thus, a portrait may capture the essence of a person more "truly" than a photograph and a wholly invented movie may portray life as it really is, showing it more accurately than the newsreel that preceded it.

This is a distinction that adults make more easily than children. Young children have difficulty in comprehending the "gray area" between truth and falsehood. They often respond with great indignation to teasing, joking and misrepresentation. In their eyes, someone who tells them something that isn't strictly true is telling a lie.

Especially around the age of six or seven, it seems, children become very upset and indignant when someone apparently believes, or wants them to believe, things that are not so. Do the Biblical stories of Noah's Ark, or the splitting of the Red Sea, fall in the same category as his little friend's story of seeing a flying horse near school?

The Bible, as we have mentioned, is not *a book* but many books. Some parts of it are history—stories of the kings of Israel and the wars they fought. These stories are substantially true, like most history. They give us an honest, accurate picture of those times and teach us that Israel was never very important as a military power or the seat of an empire. It was significant because of its religious way of life, which many more people came to appreciate later.

Other parts of the Bible are poems and they are true in the special way that poems are true. A poem tries to say something in an interesting way. If the poet who wrote the 23rd psalm says, *"the Lord is my shepherd,"* he doesn't mean that God is really a shepherd. He means that God takes care of him, tries to keep him safe from harm and makes sure that he has what to eat and drink. He says that believing in God makes him feel good and secure. We decide whether the psalm is true, not by determining whether God is really a shepherd, but by deciding whether what the poet says about God when he uses those words is true to life.

And then there are the stories, which most of the questions will probably resolve about. They stand somewhere between history and poetry, closer to poetry, and our expectations of accuracy must be different when we approach them as compared to our approach to the historical narratives. When we try to decide whether the stories are true or not, we shouldn't ask, "did it really happen this way?" as in a history lesson. Instead, we ought to ask, "is the point of this story true to life? Is this the way the world really is?" as we do with a poem. After all, none of the stories in the Bible was written by the people to whom they were supposed to have happened. We can't expect the story-teller to know what really went on and who spoke what words to whom. Neither is the author really trying to tell us what occurred a long time ago; instead, he is trying to tell us something about the kind of world we live in and the kind of people the Jews are supposed to be.

The point of the story of Creation, for example, is not
to let us know that it took six days to create the world,
or that plants were made before fish. After all, how could
the author have known this and why should we really be
interested? The meaning for us is that the world is a neat,
orderly place, where day and night, land and water are
separated, where apple seeds grow into apple trees, where
dogs have puppies, elephants baby elephants and people
baby boys and girls, a world in which people are different
from the animals because they have "a little spark of
God" inside them and so can do things which none of the
animals can do. These are the ideas that make the story
of Creation a true story. If a scientist proves that it took
millions of years and not six days, or that there is no "fir-
mament" keeping the "upper waters" from falling on us;
or if someone someday finds evidence that fish existed
before plants, the real point of the story of Genesis would
be no less true.

We very often hear or tell stories that aren't true, in
the sense that the events described never really happened
to real people and we are not lying when we tell them,
because everyone knows that they are not true in that
sense and that we are not trying to fool anyone. We read
adventure stories for excitement, although we know that
these adventures didn't happen to real people. We read
fairy tales about genies and dragons and men with magic
powers. We read myths about gods and men and creatures
who never existed, and legends about real people who
didn't really do the marvelous things described in the
stories. These stories are fascinating just the same and we

can learn a lot from them. The story of a hero who goes out to fight a dragon teaches us about courage; the dragon may be imaginary but the idea of courage is real and worth reading about. If Abraham wasn't really the man of justice and of faith that the Biblical stories represent him as being (and how will anyone ever know one way or the other? The historical Abraham is lost—only the Abraham of the narrative lives on), we can still learn much that is true about faith and justice from these stories. The moral ideas of the Biblical tales are true and valid most of the time and since we turn to the Bible essentially for moral guidance and not ancient history, the question of historical accuracy is of less importance.

Noah and the Flood

Most children find the story of Noah and the Flood a charming tale, just a bit scary, filled with animals enough for any child (if they are not permitted to bring pets into the house, they especially enjoy picturing the menagerie which inhabits the Ark at God's command), and with a happy ending. Some children are frightened at the thought of a flood destroying the whole world. If they brood about their own imperfections and penchant for doing wrong, they may take God's threat to sweep away the evildoers personally. Should our children show signs of this (and only if they do), should they become uneasy or apprehensive during the telling of the story or during a heavy rain after hearing it, should they ask us, "How would we escape if another flood came?" we might reassure them that the story of Noah and the Ark was a story people used to tell long ago in order to teach the important lesson that wicked societies don't last. There have been a lot of heavy rains since them and even many local floods, but none have even come close to wiping out all life. In fact, the Biblical story of the Flood tries to tell everybody not to worry about a flood reappearing, even if men do return to evil. It ends with a promise, symbolized by the rainbow, that there will never again be a flood so great that it will cover the world. Should our children react with apprehension, we can teach them to find reassurance in the appearance of a rainbow after the storm, even as their ancestors did long ago.

The Binding of Isaac

The story of God's commanding Abraham to sacrifice his son as a burnt offering and then stopping him at the last moment, is perhaps the most difficult narrative of all to teach children. It is the one I would be inclined to skip, if possible. I would rather try to teach the most abstruse theological claim or the most involved story of sexual relationships than this particular story, with its theme of hostile parental designs on a young child. It must be terribly frightening to a youngster to have even the possibility raised openly that his father might kill him. Adults can understand the ambivalent feelings a parent has for a child and can maintain their emotional distance from the question. Children, I suspect, are terrified.

If we can't avoid the story, we can try to make the following points:

(1) It is a very difficult story to understand. Even

grown-ups are puzzled by it.

(2) One of the points the story makes is that Abraham loves Isaac very much, that in fact he loves Isaac most of all in the world.

(3) Another major point is that God doesn't want Abraham to hurt Isaac. It is hard to believe, but there were religions at the time which taught that God wanted people to sacrifice their children. They thought human sacrifice would show that they loved God more than sacrificing money or food would show it. But this story tells how Abraham came to realize that those religions were wrong, that God definitely did not stand for parents harming their children. He opposed it. (Sometimes parents have to do things their children don't like for their long-range good. But it is *never* right for them to hurt their children to show God how much they are willing to do for Him.)

Miracles

There are events described in the Bible which strain the credulity of the reader. The Red Sea splits at just the right moment; the sun stands still for Joshua and the walls of Jericho fall at his signal. Young children respond to these stories with open-eyed wonder, delighted at this reassurance that the world conspires to safeguard the innocent and the just. At this point, there is very little to be gained by talking them out of this point of view. The best course is to avoid raising questions until our children do and then to be sure that we are ready with good answers.

My experience with religious school students indicates that around the age of eleven, children become disturbed by the improbabilities of the Biblical stories to which they have been exposed and which they have accepted virtually without question to this point. They may express this change of heart through explicit questions and complaints, such as, "How could it have happened?" Or they may betray their uneasiness by interjecting skeptical phrases between themselves and the Biblical material, "Well, it says here that..." "According to what the book says is supposed to have happened..."

In our response, we should deal with the child's uneasiness in criticizing a text he has been taught to revere even before we get to the points at issue themselves. We must emphasize that there is nothing wrong with questioning, with measuring the claims of the stories against our own logic and experience. In fact, it is a religious *obligation* to use our God-given intelligence to discover the truth. We should make the point that, while we revere the Bible and regard it seriously, we know that it was written a long time ago, when most of the scientific knowledge we now have about the world wasn't available to even the most learned of men. Its stories were written by people who didn't see the original events happen, but put into written form tales that had been in circulation over many generations. Isn't it possible that a few mistakes and exaggerations crept into the telling of an otherwise true and accurate story, details added by people who didn't know that their embellishments were "miraculous" and "impossible?"

The creators of the Bible, the men who put these wonderful stories into the forms in which we know them, took questions of truth and honesty seriously. They weren't the sort of people who would make a story up, knowing it to be false, just to impress people with God's greatness. They believed that all the things they wrote of could have happened. They believed in a God who *could* suspend or overrule the laws of Nature "if He wanted to." They saw things happen; they heard about great victories and miraculous rescues and they had no qualms about believing that God had set aside the laws of Nature for His people's sake. They didn't make the same distinctions between natural and supernatural, possible and "miraculous" that we make today. Today, after a long process of discovering how our world works, we see God in the unchanging workings of Nature, not in their suspension for our express benefit. Some aspects of Biblical narrative, which to our ancestors were no more (or less) supernatural than the healing of a wound or the ripening of an ear of grain, create a "credibility gap" for the modern reader.

How do we respond to the miraculous tales of the narrative? I think we can assume that *something* happened in them; the Jews *did* get out of Egypt, and did conquer Canaan, even if these things didn't happen precisely as described in the Bible in every detail. Something happened, and the Hebrew people tried to preserve the memory of what had happened in a exciting, impressive story whose underlying moral was that God is on the side of those who try to do what is right.

For people who lived long ago and understood the world in the light of the best scientific knowledge of the time, the most important aspect of the miracle was that God took a hand in events and made the "impossible" happen. They emphasized this aspect of the miracle when they wrote the history of those events. For us, for whom the "impossible" cannot happen and the laws of nature cannot be suspended, the important part of a miracle is that *something entirely possible happened when it didn't have to happen,* when there was no way human beings, by their own efforts, could have made it happen, and by happening, helped people go on believing in the reality of God and in the goodness of His world.

It is in this definition that we find the answer to the perennial question, "Why don't miracles happen to us today the way they used to?" The answer is that they *do* happen precisely as they used to. The "miraculous," supernatural aspects of the miracles never happened in Biblical times, any more than they do now. But things do happen "miraculously" today, when we need them and have no way to command or compel them. When they happened to a scientifically unsophisticated generation, people described them in extravagant, supernatural terms. Their truth was crusted over with a layer of misapprehension. When such events happen today, we are grateful, we find the world a friendlier and more cooperative place, but we forget that we are entitled to call them miracles. The events are no different from the ones that befell our Biblical ancestors; only the idiom in which we describe and respond to them has changed.

The point of the Red Sea story, for instance, is that when it seemed impossible for the Israelites to escape from Pharoah's chariots, God helped them to do it. The point is made in the Bible in vividly supernatural terms (you may remember the scene in Cecil B. deMille's movie "The Ten Commandments" where a ball of green fire, representing God, pushes the sea wall back) because the narrator of the story had no idea that this was less possible or more "miraculous" than any other manner of getting his heroes out of Pharoah's clutches and he wanted his story to be as impressive and as memorable as he could make it.

Similarly, the point of the story of Jericho—or the sun's standing still for Joshua—is that the Israelites later came to understand their ability to conquer and settle in Canaan, not in terms of having had an invincible army, but because God was on their side, and had made them instruments of His long-range plan for mankind. Biblical scholars have retold the story of the conquest of Canaan from a military-strategic point of view emphasizing the political disorganization of the Canaanite city-states and the relative advantages of fighting on hills and fighting in valleys. They end up with an account which is probably historically more accurate, but less edifying and less significant for us today than the one in the book of Joshua.

Are we to assume then that some of the details in the Biblical narrative are wrong and that some of the events described there never happened? That seems clearly the case. In the stories of the early history of Man and of the patriarchs, there is no problem. They are meant to be "once-upon-a-time" stories, tales bearing a moral, not lesson in geology or anthropology and we read them as tales. When we reach the story of the Israelite nation, from the Exodus onward, these inaccuracies, when they occur, are due largely to the enthusiastic, uncritical imagination of the Israelites who later told the story from generation to generation. Sometimes they succumbed to the temptation of exaggerating what God had done, because they conceived of God differently than we do today and because they believed that these fanciful deeds were things God might have done, perhaps even should have done. Sometimes they took too literally a poetic expression in the story as they heard it. An early poet may have described Joshua as hoping the day would last long enough for Israel to complete its victory, and a listener may have received and then transmitted the impression that the sun actually stood still until the fighting was over. (We are fairly certain that these stories were first rendered in poetry and then put into prose form at a later date; the key verse in the story of the sun standing still is virtually the only poetic passage in the book of Joshua.)

"Does that mean that the *Torah* is a less than perfect book?" I suppose it does. It contains inspired truths, comprehended and put into words by men, and the way men put ideas into words will inevitably be less perfect than the inspired ideas with which they started. After all, they wrote in the language of their time, for the people of their time, with only the meagre knowledge of science and history that was available to them then.

"Why do we revere the *Torah* if it's not perfect, if it's

just an old book full of mistakes? How do we know when it is right and when it's wrong?"

The Bible may not be perfect, but it is certainly not full of errors. It may get a few details wrong, but its main message—the point it is really trying to make—will usually be valid. When we read it in order to understand the kind of world we live in, to learn about what people can in fairness expect of themselves, to acquaint ourselves with examples of good and bad people, we will most often find its answers acceptable and profound.

We respect the Bible, we call it holy—not because it is a perfect book written by God, but because it is the basic document of the Jewish people, the book that describes what sort of community the Jewish people is meant to be and how we came to be that and because it has a large number of important and accurate things to say about how a person should live. Over the course of the centuries, this collection of Israel's sacred literature—despite its scientific shortcomings and historical errors—has succeeded in shaping the personality of the Jewish people. For example, it relates stories of how dedicated our forefathers were to their covenant with God. The point of these stories is less to supply us with biographical data about our forefathers than to emphasize the importance of such self-sacrificing dedication. And they have succeeded. Over the years, Jews have been shaped by the idealized values of the Bible more than by its scrupulously accurate history. The legends of Abraham and David, whether they ever happened or not, made the Jewish people become what they did, far more than did the chronologies of the kings of Judah and Israel.

We can accept the Bible as being holy, not on the basis of who wrote it, but because of what it is about and what it does for people who study it. In justifying its claim to the title, Holy Scripture, the question of whether it *leads* to holiness is more important than the question of whether it *stems from* holiness.

The "Immorality" of the Bible

Similar to problems of miracles and scientific inaccuracies, and in some ways even more troubling, is the matter of the Bible's apparent condoning of immoral behavior by its leading figures. Abraham denies that Sarah is his wife; Jacob cheats his father and brother; Joseph tattles on his brothers and they avenge themselves by selling him into slavery; King David has a man killed because he covets the man's wife. Our children read these stories, respond to the familiar family conflicts and inevitably react to the wrongness and the unfairness of many actions. How can the Bible be a book of religion and righteous living, yet ask us to admire people who do immoral things?

In another age, the Rabbis felt obliged to answer questions by justifying the behavior of their Biblical heroes. It was not for the descendants to pass judgment on their forefathers' morality, but rather to imbibe morality from them. Thus, Abraham wasn't really lying, we are told: his statement that Sarah was his sister and not his wife was accurate because of an unlikely—and hitherto unmentioned—technicality. Jacob was in fact entitled to the blessing he received and merely prevented his father from giving it to the wrong brother. King David was justified in having one of his soldiers killed in order to marry the man's wife because the man was really a traitor and deserving of death and because his wife had been promised to David when they were both children (details the Biblical narrative somehow forgot to mention.) If these answers appear ludicrous and anachronistic, I have heard each given seriously by a teacher trying to justify the Bible and keep it free from moral blemish.

I don't recommend this approach, made on the ground that the Bible and its heroes must be beyond reproach, no matter what. First of all, I cannot accept the idea that true religion *ever* asks us to turn off our moral judgment and critical intelligence. Secondly, such twisted casuistry rarely works. It only lessens our child's opinion of the Bible and of the intelligence and moral level of its defenders.

The answer to this vexing matter of Biblical morality has three facets. Firstly, the Biblical narrative introduces us to its leading characters, "warts and all." It shows them to be men of genius, inspired figures, leaders and pioneers, but human beings as well, with the faults and imperfections of any human being. Abraham was a great man, but he could still become so fearful for his own safety that he could tell a not very admirable lie to save his own skin. Isn't it important for a child to know that even a very fine man has his faults, that doing something shameful because you are afraid doesn't disqualify you from being a good person? Isn't that in many ways a more valuable lesson than being taught to admire Abraham as a man who was immune to normal human emotions?

Isaac, Jacob, Joseph, Moses, David—all had their weaknesses and the Bible never shrinks from mentioning them. But they were all great men who contributed significantly to society. *You don't have to be perfect to be good*—that is one of the most important lessons the Bible has to teach a child—about himself, his parents and teachers, his friends. A mistake, even a serious one, doesn't necessarily disqualify a person from the possibility of being a fine and decent human being.

Secondly, the Bible often describes improper behavior *without* condoning it. In most cases, following the story to its conclusion brings us to the Bible's point—that immoral behavior leads to its own punishment. Rather than cry, "Shame," and deliver a sermon about the wrongness of the deed, the narrative leads us to find its consequences for ourselves.

Take, for example, one of the most controversial examples, one to which children always respond strongly because they can well understand the sibling rivalry for a parent's affection. Isaac prefers one of his sons, Esau, to the other, Jacob, and decides to give Esau the patriarchal blessing. Isaac is an old man, nearly blind, and so Jacob is able to disguise himself as Esau, covering his arms with goatskin to appear as his hairier brother. The trick works and Isaac gives Jacob the blessing.

At this point, the typical young reader is indignant. "How could the *Torah* let him get away with it, tricking his father and cheating his brother?" The real answer lies not in a justification of what Jacob did, but in further reading of the story to discover that he doesn't "get away with it" at all.

Jacob has to leave home because Esau is angry with him. He goes to the home of his uncle Laban, tells him the whole story, falls in love with Laban's daughter, Rachel, and works seven years for the right to marry her. Then, on the wedding night, Laban substitutes Rachel's unattractive older sister for the bride, saying: "We wouldn't do such a thing here, to substitute the younger for the elder." Jacob is tricked in the same fashion he tricked his father.

Later in life, Jacob makes the same mistake his father made in prefering one of his sons, Joseph, to the others. The brothers conspire to sell Joseph into slavery and dip his coat in goat's blood to convince their father that Joseph is dead. The irony of it is not lost on the sensitive reader: as Jacob killed a goat to trick his father, so do his sons use a goat to trick their father.

The point of the story is not that Jacob did something apparently immoral and got away with it, with God's approval. The point is precisely the opposite—that you don't really get away with anything, that Jacob did something wrong and that it very definitely caught up with him.

And thirdly, in all fairness, we must admit that there are times when the Bible does seem to endorse what strikes us as immorality. It has no tears for the Canaanites who are extirpated on their land. It accepts the fact that people are struck down for the violation of some obscure ritual taboo, or simply, like the first-born of the Egyptians, for being in the path of one of God's wonders. It includes laws to protect the lot of the slave, but never suggests that slavery itself is a violation of human dignity.

There is no way to answer such charges, except to say that in these cases the *Torah* falls short of its own moral vision. The moral basis for our indignation is in the *Torah,* but for one reason or another, it was not applied in these cases. In a very real sense, the *Torah,* indeed the entire Bible, is an incomplete book. It stands at an early point in the story of man's moral development; later generations have built on it and added to it. We can say that every generation is called upon, not only to accept the *Torah* but to add new *torah* to it, to add to the Jewish people's collective understanding of how men are obliged to live.

We are always entitled to call the *Torah* to witness against itself, that is, to apply its own moral standards to some of its passages. We do it no disservice when we let it teach us the highest moral principles, standards so high that the *Torah* itself—the work of human hands and minds and the product of its own age—sometimes fails to live up to them. We show no disrespect in reading the Bible critically in this manner, providing we do it to separate the valid from the inaccurate, the permanent from the transient, not to refute the Bible's claims upon us.

Let us remember that the literature of the *Torah* and of the Bible as a whole evolved over a period of several generations. Old stories, told and retold in fixed form, old laws and customs were set into a national literature that kept on growing and evolving around them. If two places in the Bible show different levels of moral sensitivity, this is not a case of inconsistency and contradiction. It is, instead, documentary evidence of growth and maturation, of how a people who once believed and practiced a certain set of ideals grew to the point of believing and practicing another, higher set. The implication is clear: we are urged to take the *Torah* as our starting point and to continue growing in the direction in which it points us.

How and Why We Read the Bible

Most of the problems of studying the Bible are considerably reduced when we master the distinction between taking it *seriously* and taking it *literally*. We can take its message with the utmost seriousness, even if we realize that its picture of God and the universe may be misleading, its narratives often wrong in detail and its morality occasionally reflecting an earlier stage of man's moral development.

As Jews, we can and must take it seriously because it is the one book that gives us the story of the emergence of the Jewish people and the basis of the Jewish religion. The fundamental message of the Bible is that of the Jewish people's encounters with God and their commitment to becoming a special kind of community because of these encounters. It is their attempt to preserve a permanent record of the meaning of that confrontation in story, song, law, and custom. No Jew can know who he is and where he comes from until he has heard the message of the Bible.

As human beings concerned with meaningful living, we must take the Bible seriously because it represents the most thorough and valid effort to deal with meaning in life and to pass on to us the insights of inspired men.

There are those whose need for certainty and unquestionable authority leads them to make a god of the Bible and to derive from it not only their views of Man and Life, but also of physics, economics, geology, anthropology and political science. They are, understandably, upset by any suggestion of scientific misunderstanding or scribal error within its pages. But we, while honoring the Bible at least as much and taking it as seriously as they do, even while realizing that at times the Bible *is* trying to impart (incorrect) geology and anthropology, can still turn to the Bible for what it does best: the purveyal of the national-religious literature of the Jewish people, the relation of how we became a people and of what sort of people we became and the summarization of its inspired insights as to how men should live. We can let the Bible sensitize our consciences and sharpen our acumen so that we know when to respond to it and when to look beyond it.

Some Things the Bible Tells Us
(and how we might understand them)

The Bible tells us many things about God and His relationship to the Jewish people and the world. Some of them we find immensely edifying (such as the idea that God stands for Justice, Compassion, and other "divine" qualities men are called upon to develop.) Others, such as the idea that God protects the righteous and strikes down sinners, we have difficulty in accepting. Still others we put into today's terminology and imagery in order to make their meanings clear and avoid misunderstanding.

God Is One

What does it mean when we say that God is one? It doesn't mean that God is a person living in heaven and there is only one of Him there, rather than a whole family or a heavenful. Monotheism—the belief that God is one —isn't a matter of arithmetic, of counting up gods, but a statement about the *kind* of God we believe in.

"God is one" means that God is unique. Nothing or no one on earth is exactly like Him. We don't really have words, in English or any other language, to describe Him. We can talk about Him with ordinary, human words, "thing-talk," because these are the only words we have. We can speak about what He makes possible in our lives. But we must always remember that He is a little different from the ways in which we think of Him because nothing we have found on earth is precisely like Him. As human beings, we can be a little like God, because we have souls and the ability to choose to be good. But God will always be different from us and from the picture we have of Him. He is unique; neither on earth nor in heaven is there another force like Him.

"God is one" means that the *same* God exists for people everywhere. They all have the same rights and the same possibilities and they all have the same obligation to live by the same standards which are built into the world and human nature. They must do the same things to become fully and truly human.

Some people long ago believed (and some today still do) in many gods. Sometimes they saw the gods as getting along peacefully with each other, dividing the responsibility among themselves—a god of rain, god of war, god of healing and so on. Sometimes the gods were seen as quarreling among themselves and then the will of the strongest would prevail. The authors of the Bible realized that this was not a true understanding of how things happened in the world. There was so much unity, order, and coordination in the world that it had to derive from a single unifying spirit. These authors understood that certain things were absolutely right and others absolutely wrong for all people at all times and they couldn't believe that "one god says it is permitted and another god calls it forbidden and the worshipper may choose which to follow."

Other peoples believed in two gods—a good and an evil one. This explained neatly the problem of evil and suffering which resulted from moments when the "evil god" reigned supreme. Biblical religion refused to admit that there was another divine force as real and as powerful as God, a force that liberated destructive energies in the same way that God liberates creative energies. There is no Devil as a figure independent of God, as powerful as He is but evil in the Bible or in later Judaism. Human wickedness is the result of living without God or serving false gods, non-existent ones, not of serving a God of Wickedness.

The Jews Are God's Chosen People

The concept of the "chosen people" is a difficult one to grasp because it is so open to misunderstanding. As expostulated in the Bible, it clearly *does not* mean that all Jews are good and all gentiles bad. It certainly does not mean that God is the God of the Jews only and other people may not or need not turn to Him. It means that the people of Israel felt that they understood something about God, the only God of the world, more clearly than other peoples did. They had come to understand (or, as they put it, He had revealed to them) what He expected of men and how He wanted them to live in greater detail and with more clarity than had been granted any other group. Therefore it was their special responsibility to live according to those insights, to be a "pilot community" from whom all other peoples would learn of what a God-oriented life consisted.

Why did God choose the Jewish people? It is never quite clear in the Bible. Sometimes it seems due to their being the descendants of Abraham, who had a sensitivity to matters of this sort. Sometimes it seems due to Israel's being a small, insignificant people, with little military or economic power, a nation whose effect on the world would derive solely from its religious genius. Usually, the Biblical narrative abstains from trying to "read God's mind" and this would be a good example for us as well. We can no longer believe in a God who "chooses" one people, "reveals" the laws of living to them and "expects" more from them afterward. Yet it *is* an historical fact, and not just an arrogant claim, that our ancestors of the Bible *did* understand better than their neighbors what God stood for and what He wanted of men, and that it was through them that He set down a great number of new and inspired ideas about life which no one had previously comprehended.

Did this mean special privileges for the Jews? Not in the sense that they were permitted to evade anything because they were God's people. (Through much of Jewish history, the opposite view prevailed: that God demanded *more* of the Jews. This was based on the implicit assumption that the history of Israel operated under different laws than the histories of other nations— an idea we have difficulty accepting today.) We are, of course, free to demand more of ourselves than we demand of others and the Jews have often done this with eminently worthwhile results. But we can hardly deny that it is equally the "will of God" for a gentile to demand more of himself morally than he does of his neighbors.

The Significance of Everyday Deeds
(or "Why Does God Care What I Eat?")

Another one of the great and original ideas of Biblical religion, developed more fully in later Judaism, was the concept of the religious significance of the ordinary, everyday deed. Worshipping God was not confined to special times and places, though it certainly included them. It was possible to eat, sleep, dress in such a way that these ordinary activities were turned into *mitzvot*—religious deeds. That is why the *Torah* regulates the dietary habits of the Jew, commands fringes on his garment and sets patterns for many other day-to-day activities.

Throughout the ages, many people have regarded these *mitzvot* as divine calls for obedience. One heeds them as God's will, or disobeys them as an expression of divesting oneself of the yoke of His commandments. It was even suggested by some of the sages that he who performs the *mitzvot* because he appreciates their usefulness is less worthy than the man who does them simply because his "Father in Heaven" has ordained them. It's assumed that God is pleased by our obedience and either angered or disappointed by our non-observance.

Whether or not the authors of the Bible regarded daily ritual observance in this manner, today's Jews overwhelmingly do not. Hence the question our children ask, "Why should God care about what I eat? Or whether I wear a *yarmulke* at services?"

Our answer has to be that, technically, God doesn't care. We don't believe in a God who issues instructions, is flattered by compliance and angered by disobedience. We don't believe in a God who is susceptible to emotions of anger, chagrin or delight. There may be reasons for performing these religious deeds, there may even be a sense in which we "do God's will" by such observance. But the old and widespread concept that we please or anger God in our ceremonial behavior must give way to a different view.

Why then is a religious book like the Bible so involved in what people eat and the like? We have suggested that it is the purpose of religion to guide men in their development to help them to be authentic human beings, and that the term "God" stands for the sum of the forces which move us in that direction. The Bible's brilliant insight teaches that Man's spiritual development is aided by attaching religious significance to many moments of his day—waking, eating, dress, encounters with nature. Let a man regulate his breakfast, lunch and supper in a certain way and he will have three more occasions each day for affirming his membership in a "covenant community," pledged to certain purposes. He will be reminded three additional times each day that his behavior is divided into "permissible" and "forbidden" categories. Moreover, these three daily affirmations center around the act of eating, which, though it may seem mundane to some, has in fact tremendous emotional importance for the average person: for we know that eating has overtones of the infant's dependence on the world, nourishment by it and is tied to memories of early parental care.

In addition, certain forms and observances, which may have had little moral content in and of themselves, have become *sancta* of the Jewish people. That is, they have become symbols and expressions of Jewish ideals, of "the way Jews do things" in order to make a religious point. There are many ways of expressing the burdens and privileges of freedom: Jews do it by eating unleavened bread during the week of Passover. There are many ways of indicating that a special mood of concentration is appropriate for moments of prayer: Jews have devised a "uniform" of *tallit, tefillin,* and *yarmulke.* By expressing universal ideas in a specifically Jewish idiom, one affirms his commitment both to the idea itself and to the Jewish people as a vehicle for perpetuating that idea.

Post-Biblical Judaism went on to develop this "science of the sanctification of the everyday," with its immense capacity and potential for helping the ordinary individual to feel significant. Judaism let him know that his every deed could become either an act of sanctifying himself and his world or a point of rebellion against God and the *Torah.* It arranged a hundred blessings for him to recite at various moments of the day and in each of them a Jew would, in effect, be saying to himself between the lines: "I am a Jew, acting in a Jewish way. I am standing before God and expressing my gratitude for what is mine in the world."

Today, we might be less extravagant in defining the scope of this approach, but the underlying idea is one to which we should respond. It may well be "the will of God" that we multiply our opportunities for affirming that we are Jews and for attaining a gratifying sense of having performed a "religious act." The *mitzvot* of food and dress may be a kind of moral calisthenic by which we habituate ourselves to responsiveness and self-discipline, so that, on those rare occasions when great moral demands are put upon us, we will be better prepared to meet them.

Chapter VI

THE VOCABULARY OF RELIGION

Sin, *Mitzvah,* Repentance, Prayer

Conversation of two children:

"Where did you get that ring?"

"I found it."

"Well, you better find out who it belongs to, and give it back. It's a sin to keep something that doesn't belong to you."

"It's not a sin. I didn't steal it. There's no law against keeping something you find. A sin is doing something you know is wrong."

"Oh yeah? Well, there is no law against eating bread on Passover either, but that's a sin."

Every specialized field has its own technical vocabulary, a glossary of terms it has developed over the course of years to express complicated thought in a concise phrase or two. Plumbers, physicists, football players all have their own jargon, their own terms which make communication with others in their fields easier and more precise. Religion, too, has its specialized vocabulary—words like God, prayer, commandment, sin, repentance, salvation—succinct words to communicate subtle and complicated ideas. In order to achieve effective communication in a conversation, both parties must understand the terms in the same way; one of the most difficult problems in many discussions on religion is that participants often use the same vocabulary while attaching different meanings to the words.

The term "Sin," for example, means whatever we make it mean. By common consent, it has a negative connotation; it means doing something wrong. But beyond that, what does it mean? Does Sin mean disobeying God, violating one of His commandments? Does it mean doing something against the law—is Sin what "religious people" call a crime? Do you judge it subjectively—is what makes you feel guilty a sin and what leaves you with a clear conscience not? Or do you judge it by some objective code to which a person has committed himself, so that something may be a sin when done by a Catholic but not when done by an Episcopalian, or a sin when committed by a member of an Orthodox synagogue but not when done by a member of a Reform Temple?

The all-too-common concept of Sin assumes a God who has revealed His will to us in a series of specific commandments. To sin is to disobey God's will by transgressing one of His commandments and making Him angry or disappointed in us. God is likened to a parent, who sets standards, checks to see if these standards are met and stands ready to compel obedience through punishment or other means if they have not.

Up to a certain point, this concept of God and His authority is appropriate and probably inevitable. The development of the idea of God as an outside voice of authority into the idea of God as an internalized voice of commitment and conscience terminates a long process of maturation, when it comes at all. As Piaget's studies have shown, children up to the age of nine or so regard all rules as immutable and assume that they have been given by God. They believe this not only about the rules of life and behavior but about the rules for the games they play. Any suggestion, for instance, that the rules of a game of marbles be altered strikes them as an attack on the foundations of universal order: "You can't do that," they say, "that's not how it's supposed to be."

There is probably not much point in trying to give them a more sophisticated concept of commandments during this stage of their development. When they ask, "Did God tell us this is wrong?" or "Does God want us to do this?" (or more likely, when they *tell* us that "God wants us to do it") we can answer, "Yes, you're right. It is something like that. These are some of the things that God wants us to understand are wrong. Of course, you know that God doesn't have a mouth to tell us things, the way ordinary people do, because God is different from people. But He has let people know that these things are wrong, even if we sometimes feel like wanting to do them. But by listening to God, we won't do them and feel sorry afterward."

This applies to a case where we want to enforce the commandment in question and only want to be sure that the origin of that obligation is not too drastically misunderstood. If there is a religious or moral usage we would just as soon not have our children take seriously, we might say: "You understand that nobody knows *exactly* what God has told us to do, because He doesn't have a mouth to talk with, as people do. God is different from people. But God has given us minds and consciences and religious leaders in every generation, to help us understand what is right and what is wrong. Some people have used the minds that God gave them and decided that this is something they have to do. But your parents, and the religious leaders we have spoken to, have thought a lot about it and we don't feel that God expects this of us. Like a lot of things in religion, this is a question people are still working hard at to understand."

One thing we should always strive to avoid is a concept of sin which is guilt-producing. We might say: "No, God won't get angry with you if you do something wrong. He won't punish you for it, and He won't be disappointed in you. You will probably be a little bit angry with yourself, because you don't like to be a person who does wrong things and so you will probably want to do something extra nice to make up for it. But God won't be angry at you, because as we understand God, He doesn't have feelings of that sort."

Assuming that young children conceive of God as a magnified parent, this answer will be accepted more readily by a child if his own parents are not enraged by disobedience, driven to distraction by mistakes and failures, and do not respond punitively to what the child does wrong.

Commandment

When a child gets beyond assuming that the way things are done is the way they must be done (around age 10, according to Piaget's experiments with marble players), we can speak to him of sin and commandment in different terms. Commandments need no longer be the edicts of a God-person living in Heaven; neither are they simply rules men have agreed upon for their mutual convenience and benefit. We might say to our slightly older children:

"The purpose of life is to grow to be the very best person you can.

"The purpose of religion is to help you grow to be the very best person you can by sharing with you what the greatest souls of the past have learned about living and by helping you associate with other people who want the same things out of life that you do.

"A commandment is something you ought to do, so that you will grow to be a better person. (Sometimes the commandment tells you what you have to avoid doing.) Some commandments tell you to do things which are very important. Others tell you to do things which aren't so important, but help you to form good habits for later in your life.

"We speak of commandments as being 'the will of God' because God is what we call the feeling in us and in the world that guides us in growing to be good and makes it possible. But even though we talk that way, we should not make the mistake of thinking of God as a person who tells us to do certain things and doesn't like us if we don't do them. We should do these things because they help us become the sort of people we want to be."

Sin

If performing a commandment means doing one of the things which helps a person grow and be all he ought to be, committing a sin would then mean failing to do such a thing. A sin would be a *missed opportunity* to do something which would have made us better people and which would have helped others.

The Hebrew word for sin, *chet,* comes in fact from a root meaning "to miss the target," though the Biblical conception of sin is more a matter of disobedience and violation than of missed opportunity for self-fulfilment. The Hebrew religious vocabulary has several words for sin expressing different degrees of seriousness. The Biblical prophets, especially, had a rich vocabulary of words with which to characterize the people's misdeeds. Some of the things the people did were relatively minor examples of squandered opportunities to improve themselves. Some were weak-willed concessions to temptation. Others were deliberate acts of rebellion against God and rejection of His goals and reached the point of diminishing the divine image we represent. There were advantages in this breadth of vocabulary. Discussions of observance and transgression, with adults as well as with children, often run into difficulty because we tend to use the same word, "sin," when we refer to minor deviations in ritual and major immoralities alike. How can any serious religion set an inadvertent violation of the Sabbath in the same category as the deliberate injuring of another human being and call them both "sin?"

To avoid the confusion caused by this usage, we must

be very careful not to use the word "sin" loosely or in-discriminately, lest we distort its meaning by overuse. If we insist on calling all sorts of trivial misdeeds "sins," we teach our children to think of "sin" as trivial. We are better off telling our children that there are a lot of things which are worth avoiding, but that some are more serious than others. There is the obvious distinction be-tween the deed which hurts someone else and the deed which hurts no one else, even though it lets an opportunity for self-improvement and Jewish affirmation go by. (This is very close to, but not quite the same as, the distinctions between ethical and ritual *mitzvot*. I would rather not put it that way, because I think it strengthens an all too prevalent tendency to play down the importance of ritual.) There is a further distinction between the "sin" whose ill effects can be redressed and the deed which, once done, holds no possibility of being undone. We can make a further distinction between the worthwhile deed for which the opportunity comes once and rarely—if ever-again, and the deed which will offer itself again and again as a possibility.

Let our children learn then, that religion uses the word "sin" to cover many kinds of misbehavior from the very serious to the very trivial. All are worth keeping away from, but some are more serious than others. We should use the word "sin" to refer, for the most part, to seriously wrong behavior, actions which hurt other people, or for which reparation cannot be made. Violations of reli-gious rules which hurt no one are not "sins," in this sense, though you will sometimes hear people call them that and though they are still worth avoiding; they are better described as "mistakes," missed opportunities for bringing ourselves closer to being the sort of people we would like to be. Again, let us emphasize that becoming a good, self-disciplined, sensitive person is very close to a full-time job: though we call certain deeds "mistakes," and acknowledge that they are not as serious as sins which hurt or endanger, they still need to be thought of with seriousness.

What happens to a person who commits a sin? First of all, having committed a sin doesn't make him a sinner with a capital "S." It doesn't condemn him as a bad person. As we have pointed out, the Bible goes out of its way to show us that its greatest heroes fell short of perfection. They all sinned at one time or another, and each of them had to work hard at overcoming the weakness that led him to do wrong.

Sometimes when we sin, we hurt another. The commandment we disobey is one involving respect for another person's feelings or property. A proper atonement would involve attempts to apologize and compensate for the damage if possible.

Often, when we sin, we feel bad about it afterwards. Even if not afraid of punishment, we are disappointed in ourselves. We really do believe in the image of the good man presented by Judaism and don't like to think of ourselves as weak or selfish. How do we make up for a sin when there is no one to whom we can apologize, when we have hurt only ourselves, for example, or when we have spoken disparagingly about a whole group of people and can't apologize to each and every one of them? Well, we might try to make a special attempt to do good, to do something unselfish—not because it will "make up" for the wrongdoing, but because it will reassure us that there are strong, self-sacrificing elements in us as well. We should avoid the "book-keeping" mentality that tells us a certain quantity of good deeds and contributions to charity "balance" or "cancel out" a certain number of the wrong things we do. But we should appreciate the need of a person who is disappointed in himself to re-assure himself of the better, nobler side of his nature.

A child who has done wrong wants to "make up for it," not necessarily because he believes that a "deposit" of good deeds cancels his debt to God and to Judaism, but because he wants to feel he is capable of doing what is right as well as what is wrong and because his instinctive sense of world harmony leads him, on a level he probably can't put into words, to feel very uncomfortable when he thinks that the world is "off balance" because the bad deeds have not been offset by good ones. The biggest mistake we can make at a time like this is to forbid him an opportunity to "make it up," or to tell him that it isn't necessary, leaving him with an image of himself as a wrongdoer, an image uncorrected by a more recent experience of himself as a "right-doer."

The greatest danger in the sins we commit, however, whatever the form or degree, lies in the danger that we will habitually disregard God's standards. The *Talmud*, in the "Ethics of the Fathers," noted long ago that just as one good deed leads to another, one sin leads to another—and that the reward of the good deed is that it makes the next good deed easier, just as the punishment for a sin is that it makes another sin more likely. We form habits; we begin to get a picture of ourselves as people who have certain weaknesses: the more regularly and repeatedly we do something, the firmer a part of our mental image of ourselves the habit becomes. Every action we perform becomes a precedent for dealing with a similar situation in the same way—unless something happens within us to make us change.

Repentance

This, too, is the meaning of Repentance in Jewish thought and in the vocabulary of Judaism. Repentance is not, as is so often assumed, a matter of regret for something we have done, sorrow for having done it or for the consequences of having done it. It is more than saying, "I'm sorry," more than actually *being* sorry. The Jewish concept of Repentance, *Teshuva,* means a *re-making of the self,* a new ordering of priorities, so that something which seemed irresistibly important to us before is now seen as much less important and so that we can henceforth respond to similar situations differently. Repentance means becoming virtually a new person in terms of our values and priorities and therefore it means that we need no longer be burdened by the guilt and shame of things we did earlier. That is why the classic test of repentance in Judaism resides in finding yourself in the same situation to which you had formerly responded weakly, "sinfully," and meeting it differently this time—because your understanding of what you stand for as a person has changed.

What, after all, makes a person a person? Not his physical appearance—height, weight, hair-color. He can change all of those and still be the same person. His personality, his sense of values, what he enjoys, how he responds to things that happen to him—these make him the person he is. *Teshuva,* repentance, means changing our values, altering our patterns of response, the way we allocate our time and thus it means becoming *new people,* not burdened by the bad habits of the past.

Salvation, Redemption, Fulfillment

"Salvation" and "Redemption" are terms not often met in Jewish thought. They are much more prominent in Christian theology; Jews for the most part don't see themselves in a condition from which they must be saved or redeemed. But if we take Salvation to mean the goal and end-purpose of life, there is a Jewish equivalent, which is not Salvation—rescue from a dire situation—but Fulfilment, making the most of an incomplete situation. Jews of an earlier age spoke of "meriting a place in *Olam Haba,* the world to come," as the goal to which their lives were dedicated. Every deed was to be evaluated in the light of whether it increased or decreased the chances of meriting that reward. We can call our own sense of where we are headed, our understanding of Fulfilment as the purpose of our lives, another sort of *Olam Haba,* world to come. As we understand it, the purpose of life is:

To realize all of our potential as human beings and

develop those God-like qualities which are latent in each of us.

To live in such a way that our influence and our memory will live on beyond our own time.

To leave the world a better, happier, more human place for having been part of it.

To live thusly is to find Fulfilment or Salvation, the purpose of our lives.

Messiah

Today, few people still look for a person, called the Messiah, to appear and change the world. Even people who conceive of God as a person have for the most part either dropped the concept of Messiah from their working vocabulary of religious ideas or graduated to a more sophisticated understanding of the term. If the idea comes up at all, it will probably be in connection with a Christian friend's claims or remarks about the Messiah having come or a Messianic reference in an old Jewish legend or prayer.

We might explain that once people thought that a savior would appear on earth, a person so good and so powerful that he would make the world a better place all by himself. This hope was prevalent at a time when one person, the king, did control the lives of the people. (The word Messiah is a Hebrew word meaning "the king, the anointed one." Originally the Messianic anticipation was simply the hope for a king who would be more honest and more effective than the kings to whom people were accustomed. As the problems of oppression and war became too great for a better-than-average ruler to solve, people began to conceive of the Messiah as having superhuman powers.) Looking forward to the coming of the Messiah was a way of expressing hope that one day the world would improve and be perfected.

Today, no one person has enough power to solve the world's problems all by himself, no matter how good, how wise or how powerful he is. We look forward, not to a man who will arrive and take care of all our problems for us, but to a Messianic Age, when all people will agree on what the world needs and change themselves to bring about that sort of world . We await a time when they will come together to solve their problems. References to the Messiah or the Messianic Age in our prayers are a way of saying that we still believe the world will improve, that people have the power within themselves to improve it.

Prayer

The idea of prayer is difficult to understand and explain when one thinks of God as we have suggested. If God were a Superperson living in Heaven, it would be easy enough to understand why we pray to Him and what we pray for. In fact, most people who believe in prayer seem to have just such a conception of God. They may not ask why they pray, but they run into the more serious problems of why deserving prayers are not answered, why God needs their flattery or their information and why certain hours and formulations of prayer find special favor in His sight.

We, who cannot conceive of God as a person and who

reject the idea that our prayers will influence events beyond our control, must find reasons for prayer, other than the belief that we are "telling God what is in our hearts."

Let us begin by drawing some distinctions. We must distinguish first between *prayer* and *worship*. Worship is any form of putting ourselves in contact with God—with the Spirit that guides us to human fulfillment. We may worship through study, through deeds of kindness and helpfulness, through an act of self-control, through charity and we may worship in many other ways. Prayer is worship through the use of words.

We must distinguish further between personal, private prayer and public congregational prayer. They are two very different modes—so different in fact that it is almost misleading to use the same term for both of them, though both are verbal forms of worship.

One of the chief purposes of congregational worship is to strengthen the feeling of being part of a congregation. At public services, we bring people together who share the same values and purposes. This is what the words "synagogue" and "congregation" mean. In a congregation people renew dedication to their purposes. Each congregant is given reassurance that he is not alone, that many other people feel as he does about the world and what it might become. Each worshipper experiences a sense of being part of a larger group which was in existence—dedicated to these same values—long before he was born, and will continue striving for them even after his life has ended. Affirmation of the congregation's dedication to common goals and values is what public prayer is chiefly about. This is why it takes place at regular hours, through the recitation of a common liturgy. Jews congregate for prayer on Friday nights and Saturday mornings, not because God keeps "office hours" then, but because being in one place at the same time is one of the central purposes of their prayer and because the Sabbath is one of the religious values they hold in common.

When individuals pray, at home or in a hospital waiting room or wherever they may be, it is a very different matter. The prayer of someone in danger who prays that he will come through it safely, the prayer of a man that God cure someone of a serious illness, are really not so much prayers as cries of pain, cries for help, which we utter not so much because we actually expect help but because we cannot help uttering them. If an airplane is going to crash, it won't be saved by our prayers. If a person is to be saved from a disease, he will be saved because of a combination of medical skill, good luck, and his own stamina and attitude, not because of any words we recite outside of his hearing. At best, as we have suggested, his knowledge that we are concerned may encourage him and strengthen his will—nor do I minimize the effect this can have on his recovery. But our words neither heal broken bones nor make malignancies vanish.

It is not wrong to offer such prayers, firstly, because people can't really help uttering them in their desperation and secondly, because they teach us one of the important lessons of authentic prayer—the awareness of our human limitations. One of the reasons we pray, in placid times as well as in times of difficulty, is to express the fact that there are things we need for our lives which we cannot get through our own efforts. We must rely on that beneficent force in the universe which makes our living fully human. Prayer is the recognition and expression of that dependence more than it is a way of influencing that force to do something additional for us.

For What Can We Pray?

We must avoid the "Santa Claus" mentality which presents God with a shopping list of our desires. What we do when we pray is express the hope that our lives will be marked by the presence of those qualities we consider divine, the wish to act justly, practice compassion, speak the truth and build peace. We acknowledge in prayer that we depend on God for all these qualities, that though we have them in potential, we need the sustaining force we call God actually to practise them in our lives.

We express in prayer our gratitude for these qualities in ourselves and in the world around us. (Despite the common conception that prayer is "asking," Jewish prayer contains much more praise than petition.)

Thus, it is proper to pray for the power to learn and to remember to be grateful when we find ourselves capable of learning, but it is not proper to pray for an "A" in next week's exam. It is our responsibility to apply the power to learn to our assignments.

To our children, we might explain prayer as "hoping that, when you try your hardest to do something you think is important, you find in yourself the ability to do it and when you do find it, being grateful for it. We pray for what we want to become—not what we want to be given."

I know some religious educators who are dissatisfied with the familiar nighttime ritual of invoking God's blessing on a long list of relatives, friends, and pets. (If they are worthy of God's blessing, would God be less inclined to bless them if the child left them out? Or does God need this testimony as to their goodness? If something bad happens to them on the following day, does this reflect on the sincerity or worth of the child who offered the prayer, or on the deserving nature of the person he prayed for?) Instead, these educators suggest the following thoughts for children: "Think of the nicest thing that happened to you today. Think of how good you felt at that moment. And let *that* be your bedtime meditation tonight." Prayer before we retire for the night thus becomes an affirmation of the world's goodness and helpfulness and recollection of its smiling face, not a matter of asking God to carry out our errands.

Why Prayers Are Not Answered

There is a quip which some of my colleagues seem to appreciate more than I do: "God always answers your prayers, but sometimes His answer is No." This strikes me as bad theology and bad psychology to boot. What do we accomplish by saying to ourselves, and to our children, that the things we prayed for were possible but that we didn't deserve them? "God could have sent you a puppy but He decided not to." "God could have saved

Daddy from sickness, as you prayed, but He had His reasons for not doing it." Does such an answer increase either our affection for God or our respect for ourselves? It would be better to remember that a prayer is not a request and that, most of the time, our prayers require no answer. If we hope for sunshine on the day of our outing and the sun does shine, it is not because "our prayers have been answered" any more than showers would indicate our unworthiness. Rain and clear skies are matters of meteorology, not morality.

In fact, no prayer which treats of changes in the world outside is ever really "answered." Only when we pray for a change *within* ourselves is it possible for our act of prayer to influence the results. For the members of a football team to pray that they play to the limits of their ability, that their minds be free of tension and distraction on the day of the big game, is perfectly appropriate. For them to pray that the other team plays badly is not only mean-spirited, but even worse, ineffective. And the fan watching the game on television, praying for his team's victory, should be under no illusion that his invocations of Heavenly aid will affect the score in any way.

Only the man who prays about what sort of person he wants to become, the man who prays for clarity of understanding and strength of purpose, has a chance of getting a response to his prayer. He invokes not the "Father in Heaven," who evaluates all of his requests and stamps each of them "Yes" or "No," but his own better self, and if he prays sincerely, the answer may be close at hand.

Chapter VII

SOME AFFIRMATIVE WAYS OF MEETING GOD

"If you would know God, be not therefore a solver of riddles. Rather look about you and you shall see Him playing with your children. And look into space; you shall see Him walking in the cloud, outstretching His arms in the lightning and descending in the rain. You shall see Him smiling in flowers, then rising and waving His hands in trees." (K. Gibran, *The Prophet.*)

God, where shall I find Thee, whose glory fills the
universe?
Behold, I find Thee
Wherever the ploughman ploughs his furrow through the
hard soil,
Wherever the quarryman pounds the stone to gravel,
Wherever man earns his bread by the sweat of his brow.
In the company of the friendless, the afflicted, the lowly,
lost,
There God abides in sun and shower.

Behold, I find Thee wherever the mind is free to follow
its own bent,
Wherever words come out from the depth of truth,
Wherever men struggle for freedom and right,

Wherever the scientist toils to unbare the secrets
of nature...
Behold, I find Thee in the merry shouts of children at play,
In the lullaby the mother sings, rocking her baby to sleep,
In the slumber that falls on the infant's eyelids,
And in the smile that plays on his sleeping lips...
(From the *Reconstructionist Prayerbook*)

The Passover *Haggadah* speaks of four types of sons. Three of them ask questions—inquisitive, skeptical, or naive questions—and the parent is instructed how to answer them apppropriately. The fourth asks no questions and his parents are told: *"You bring the matter up and find a way to give him the answers."*

Until now, we have dealt with the questions a child might ask about God, questions arising from his curiosity about the world, his experiences with disappointment and suffering and his encounters with stories and references to God in the culture around him. The most effective teaching comes, of course, when the child himself raises a question and is receptive to an answer. Our best answers will do less good and our worst will do less harm if they are offered as answers to questions no one is asking—unsolicited sermons on the nature of the universe.

Our discussion is incomplete without a discussion of how we can arrange for our children to have "God-experiences," to encounter the divine in their lives and to identify it as the divine—with the initiative on our part rather than on theirs. If we want to lead our children to a mature view of God and to sensitize them to Him, there

are times when we must point out His presence without
waiting for our children to ask.

Finding God in the World

God is the Power which makes it possible for us to
become fully human. As such we find Him in the beauty
and orderliness of Nature and in our own ability to respond
to that beauty and to understand and use that orderliness.
When we are moved by the sight of the ocean, by a rainbow, a field of flowers, the sun shining on a green expanse
of grass, we become aware not only of the beauty of the
world, but of our uniquely human capacity to enjoy and
be moved by beauty. When, safely inside our homes, we
find ourselves strangely fascinated by the fury of a bliz-
zard or the awe-inspiring power of a thunderstorm, we
(like the author of the 29th Psalm) are sensing something
about the smallness of man and his power in this great
world; but at the same time, we sense the uniqueness of
man in his ability to observe, meditate on and respond
to the world. A feeling of awe in response to the grandeur
of nature is one of the forms of religious experience our
children experience. And certainly the generation that has
seen man's first steps into the world beyond our planet
should be sensitive to the presence of God in the vastness
and orderliness of the universe, and His presence in the
minuteness—and at the same time the immense creative
capacity—of Man.

God makes Himself real in the world through growth,
change and improvement. When our children see plants
and flowers grow, when they are aware of their own

maturation, we can point to God as making this possible. We can teach them to marvel at the fact that in a tiny, inert seed lies buried the secret of life, the mystery that will one day make it a large and certain kind of plant. And when they are old enough to understand human conception and birth, we can teach them that God makes it possible for human beings—out of love for life and for each other—to create life.

A visit to the sea-shore can move a young child to go through one of man's oldest religious experiences— the fascination with the waves and with the incoming tide, the fear that the waters will inundate the earth and finally the grateful relief when he realizes that the waves will reach only so far and no farther. We can tell our children that people long ago felt exactly as they when they stood on the shore and of how our ancestors told stories in which the world was originally covered completely by water (scientists tell us this may well have been the case). We can explain how God made special places for the water to gather, so that dry land could appear. And we can point out to our children that our forefathers thanked God for having made a line beyond which the waves would not pass so that the dry land would be a place where animals and men could live. We can show how we live in an amazingly regular world, where the moon and the tides, the sunrise and the seasons, follow very precise patterns and are always just where they are supposed to be.

When a child bruises himself and learns that his bruise heals (after considerable uncertainty, the first few times, as to whether the pain or cut will ever go away), we can teach him to appreciate God for giving us the power to heal as well as to grow.

Finding God in People

It is inevitable that the young child, if he hears the word God at all and thinks about Him at all, will conceive of Him as being very much like the important adults in his world. There is no point in trying to fight this, or to force seven-year-olds to be comfortable with abstractions. But we can have some say in determining what sort of God children picture and what qualities they attribute to Him because in time these concepts will determine the kind of world in which they believe.

A child who is blessed with loving, trusting parents —parents who make it clear to him that they accept and cherish him—will begin by believing in a God who loves and accepts, in a creative spirit which is behind an essentially friendly world; he will progress to feeling at home in a world which he will view positively. A child whose parents have reasonable, consistent expectations of him will believe that he has obligations to God and to the world and that these obligations are within his capacity to fulfill.

Parents who nag, complain, over-react and over-protect will teach a child to believe in a God Who makes impossible demands and who rejects and punishes people arbitrarily and unfairly for not fulfilling them. The child's religion will be compulsive, guilt-ridden and will revolve around the avoidance of punishment rather than the achievement of positive goals. Children of this sort tend to become adults who say of God, in abject self-contempt or with thinly-veiled resentment: "He can do whatever He wants to us—who are we to question Him?"

A child is more likely to accept the reality of God as a supporting, accepting, inspiring force in the world if his own experiences with adults (parents, teachers, clergy, coaches and scout leaders) have been satisfying ones. A child who has learned that he can rely on the adult world for love, patience, and honesty will grow up to relate to God in the same way.

A child's belief in God is not a theological proposition but a readiness to trust the world, to assume that it will play fair with him. Disbelief for a young child is not philosophical atheism, but suspicion, withdrawal, surliness and fear—the reaction of a human being who has too often seen the world, his limited world, dash his hopes and expectations. (Ultimately, the child will have to learn that the world is often cruel and unfair and that many of his wishes will not be satisfied. If he has formed the basic habit of liking and trusting the world and if he is surrounded by adult models who go on believing in the world despite their own disappointments, he will survive this crisis in the evolution of his faith.)

If a child's parents find time for him, share relaxed meals, story-hours and bedtime moments with him, instead of rushing to their own concerns or grunting responses from behind their newspapers, the child will picture God in their image, a God who is concerned with the deeply-felt needs of little people. While this is an anthropomorphism he will have to outgrow, it will be a source of security and a force for affirming the world as a good and loving place during the early years.

The people in a child's world make God and the qualities for which He stands more credible. The joy of friendship, the lively satisfaction of liking and being liked, the sense of missing someone and of being missed, the capacity to be happy in interpersonal contact and to make others happy—all of these can be identified as stirrings of the force we call God in a child's soul.

Another important area in which children can discover God through other people is their exposure to, and fascination with, heroes—men of courage and dedication. Why does an explorer want to find out what some remote corner of the world is like? How does he remain brave in the face of enemies and bad weather, persevering until he reaches the worthy goal on which he has set his sights? This is God at work in a human soul. What makes a doctor risk his life and health to find the cure for some disease, trying one experiment after another? Again, this is God at work.

Heroes of faith in the Bible, giants of learning and dedication in Jewish history, great patriots, athletes displaying grace under pressure and subordinating themselves to the needs of the team, victims of misfortune overcoming disaster to lead useful lives: one vivid biography will do more than a dozen sermons to convince a child that God is real by introducing him to people in whose lives God has been a real and unmistakable influence. Courage, self-sacrifice, determination and a host of other divine qualities become part of his world in this way. Thus he is provided with God-oriented, God-affirming models, identities to "try on" during his hero-worshipping years.

Finding God in Oneself

Since a growing child spends more time thinking about himself than about any other subject, it would be advisable to habituate him to finding God when he looks into his own heart and soul. Let us show him the qualities which we believe God stands for and as he encounters these qualities in his own life God will become that much more real.

The ability to grow—physically and spiritually—comes from God, as do the healing and recovery from illness. The healthy use of our limbs, the joy of running and climbing are examples of God at work in us (a concept that is conspicuous in the opening blessings of the Jewish morning service.) The ability to improve, to be a little better than you were last week, is another manifestation of godliness. As a child learns self-control, as he learns to refrain from doing things which are tempting but wrong—at first because he wants the approval of his parents and later to satisfy his own conscience—he can feel God at work in him, giving him strength he didn't have before and enabling him to feel pleasure in the exercise of this new strength.

As a child learns things, as the jumble of alphabet-forms becomes intelligible to him, as he learns arithmetic, history, batting-orders or the species of dinosaurs, he finds God in his ability to learn and to derive pleasure from the learning process. He may not know that the prayerbook contains blessings which thank God for our ability to learn, but he knows the feeling that inspired the blessing.

God is described in the first verse of the Bible as the creative force behind the world: the power to create, to impose order where none existed and to bring forth recognizable form where none was there before, making men creatures "in the image of God." When a child creates, when he shapes a formless lump of clay into a figure, when he puts paint on paper and a picture results, when he writes a poem, he finds God within himself. At this point, we can say to the child that to believe in God means to take seriously all of the abilities which are so important to him: the ability to grow, to heal, to learn, to improve, to create. These are things God enables him to do so that he can become a real and complete person and find life enjoyable and fulfilling.

As a child learns the satisfying feeling of heeding his inner voice of conscience, as he comes to enjoy the good feelings of sharing and helping, God becomes real to him as the Source of these feelings. Self-concern is so much a full-time preoccupation of young children that at first they share only grudgingly and under coercion. But they soon reach an age when they find sharing satisfying— either for our smiles of approval or for the authentic inner feeling of doing something noble and good. We might interpret this "inner smile of the heart" for them, not as their having made God happy but as God having made *them* happy. We can show them how God has given them the ability to share so that they can choose to use it for their own benefit and that of others.

We can provide the opportunities for them to get this feeling. We can ask for charity and discuss where the money might go, we can ask them to help us in the performance of good deeds so this way of encountering God becomes a regular part of their life.

If a child has a pet for whose care he is responsible, this can be a very useful framework for his discovery of God. Through caring for the pet, he can appreciate the "parents' side" of the parent-child relationship. He can learn what it feels like to take care of someone, not only have the feeling of being taken care of. He can feel what it is like to be concerned for another's well-being and health, not only out of deflected self-concern ("What will become of me if anything happens to mommy?") but out of love. Compassion, concern, responsibility are all aspects of the divine, qualities we need to develop if we are to be fully human: this is a way for a child to start.

To understand God—not by talking about Him but by "imitating" Him, by living up to the qualities for which He stands—is an old and valid Jewish idea. If we can get a child to practice compassion, generosity, honesty, forgiveness, perseverance and to find satisfaction in them, we will make the "little bit of God" within him a very real part of his world.

Finding God in Religion

Encountering God in organized religion may be the hardest way of all, because so much of institutional religion—howsoever its adherents actually conceive of God—pictures Him as a Person living in Heaven, a Person Who listens to our prayers and judges us by the degree to which we have obeyed His commands. We may recognize this conception as poetic and metaphoric language, but many adults—let alone children—are inclined to take it literally. Practicing the wrong rituals for the wrong reasons, attending the wrong services on the wrong basis can undo much of the good this book has tried to do. It confuses a child to find authoritative spokesmen for his own religion saying that God is indeed what we have painstakingly tried to teach that He is not.

Proper public and private religious expression can add a dimension to a child's encounters with God which he would get nowhere else. Being part of an adult group expressing serious things in a formal, stylized manner can have an awesome impact on a child. If adults take a religious service seriously, the mood communicates itself to the child. In fact—given the child's natural openness to the dramatic—it becomes even more serious for him.

A feeling of awe should certainly be part of a child's education in finding God. He may get this feeling from a sunset, a thunderstorm, a mountain. But he can and should get it as well from the atmosphere of a worship service—putting on a *tallit,* seeing the Ark opened, kissing the *Torah,* hearing the congregants' voices joined in chorus. These may have little direct connection with God or with theological principles, but they will do much to cultivate a child's awe-filled response to moving moments and to show him more effectively than any logic a realm of profound meaning. The excitement of seeing the Ark opened and of touching the mantle of the *Torah* is sufficient for a child; we do not at that moment have to raise the question of the origin of the Scroll's contents.

In a home where the Sabbath candles are lit, and a traditional Friday evening is observed, young children eagerly enter into the routine. Again, this has little to do with theology, but a lot to do with helping a child to make room in his life for "special moments" and the feelings about the world which they evoke. These traditions serve the additional purposes of strengthening his ties to his family, as together they share the ceremonial routines, as well as cementing his relations to the Jewish people.

If we want to raise our children to welcome religious feelings, they should see us in attitudes of reverence—at prayer, reciting blessings, bestowing blessings upon them—so that reverence and religious solemnity become real to them, not just abstractions. They should hear us express awe and wonder, affirm faith and courage in the face of disapointment and then they will be more inclined to make those attitudes part of their own spiritual repertoire.

Parents often underestimate the child's ability to appreciate the stylized, the ceremonial. They may have tried to make him sit through a synagogue service or some other ceremony which overtaxed his capacity for sitting still, and assumed that he was "too young to get anything out of it." Actually, a child with his God-given enthusiasm and curiosity, will be very deeply impressed by the solemn, by special moments and special uniforms—within the limits of his attention span and if he is not nagged to behave at a prematurely adult level. (Children are much less skilled than adults at putting up with something banal because it is "good for them"—when it comes to religion, I'm not sure we should work at developing that particular skill.)

Children respond to Sabbath, *Hanukkah* and *Havdalah* candles, to a Passover Seder and a *Purim* noisemaker, much earlier and more enthusiastically than they do to the abstract ideas behind the observances. What do rituals do for children, especially the ones which call for their participation—lighting candles with mother, asking the Four Questions at the *Seder?* Rituals add excitement and drama to their lives and give them a feeling of being important in the world of important things, a world their parents take seriously.

I would imagine that, for the average reader of this book, the oldest and most vivid and pleasurable Passover thoughts are of a *Seder* meal with special foods, many relatives, and strange rituals—bewildering but enjoyable. We may not have understood what was going on, but we knew instinctively that it was "Jewish," it was religious and that it was familial. We owe our children similar experiences and the bases for similar memories.

The problem of training children to recite rote prayers is easy to mishandle. Prayers like the ones seen in cartoons —the child on his knees at bedside asking God to bless certain people—raise misleading expectations, and such prayers as might arise spontaneously from a child's mind —for a bicycle or a sunny day—are as bad. I would never try to force a child into the habit of daily prayer (one more thing to feel guilty about if he skips it or finds it pointless). I suggest the approach mentioned in the previous chapter, a nightime thought about "the nicest thing that happened to me today," not necessarily every night (compulsively) unless the child enjoys it. Let him get into the habit, but let us not press it on an unwilling child. If our child has picked up the "God bless Mommy, Daddy, Billy and Rover" habit from friends or TV programs, we might suggest substituting: "I'm happy to have mommy, daddy, etc... and I know they are happy to have me," and explain that this is a clearer way of saying the same thing.

Another variety of prayer we might encourage without demanding it, is the blessing of thanks for something we appreciate. Sometimes we won't have to suggest it. A child's gasp of delight at seeing the ocean on a sunny day is a blessing recited with at least as much authentic religious fervor as the benediction of an Orthodox Jew reciting the prescribed words for that occasion. If we can teach our children to be grateful rather than to take everything for granted, if we can teach them to thank God and His world for good food, new clothes and sunny days, not because God needs our words but because we want to be appreciative, this is a real contribution to their religious growth.

Some educators object to children's usage of traditional Hebrew blessings over food and new things on the grounds that it is hypocritical to recite prayers we do not understand. It seems to me that there may well be advantages in the Hebrew. Aside from their being traditional, Hebrew prayers have a quality of distinctiveness because they are in a special language designed for special times. A child will understand the thought he is trying to express, or the mood to which the prayer leads him, though he might take an English translation too literally since he thinks that he understands the words.

Beyond this, the use of Hebrew binds him to Jews all over the world who express themselves in the same language of worship and ties him to generations past as well. Using Hebrew to express the religious ideas of Judaism helps these ideas to stand out as specifically Jewish ideas and teaches a child that he belongs to the Jewish people, an old and honorable people, and that he shares this Jewish identity with people in many lands.

Here, as in virtually every subject we have touched on, we begin, *not with what God demands but with what we would like to become*—we and our children. We begin, not with doctrine or theology, but with life, with the feelings and experiences of our children. We do not start by pretending that we stand with God and calling our children to climb up and join us. We start with our children and try to see the world through their eyes, try to share with them the two most important ideas we hold: the commitment that man's greatest advenure is to be found in the never-ending striving to become fully human and the faith that if they look at the world and look into themselves deeply enough, they will find God in both.

* * *